SECRETS
at The
BIG
HOUSE

Overcoming The Damage
Of A Narcissistic Mother And
An Emotionally Absent Father

(Lessons in Resilience)

Ana Maria Michelena, MD

Table of Contents

To the Universidad Central de Venezuela, in gratitude, for the immeasurable gift of education, which saved me, and gave me the freedom and the power to fly away.

To all those whose parents failed to protect them when they were children.

To Patrick A. Devine, for believing in me.

About the Author

Dr. Michelena is the Director of Cardiac Anesthesiology at Aventura Hospital and Medical Center, a level two trauma center and a teaching institution in Aventura, Florida. She is also faculty at HCA/Kendall Regional Medical Center. Formerly, she was Chief Resident at University of Miami/Jackson Memorial Hospital. Dr. Michelena graduated magna cum laude from medical school at Universidad Central de Venezuela. She is an avid physical fitness enthusiast and mother of a precious 15-year old son.

Foreword

This is not a traditional self-help book.

The lessons learnt here are immersed within my story.

I have always loved the gift of language, writing and story-telling for the power it holds to educate, inspire and bring hope.

As a child I survived abandonment, rejection and abuse in the hands of the adults in my life.

Faith and resilience helped me transform all my painful experiences into a silent, yet powerful source of deep strength and perseverance.

My mission is to be a facilitator for the healing and uplifting of all those whose parents, in one way or another, failed to protect them when they were children.

I want to empower those who share an experience of having grown up in dysfunctional, emotionally wounding environments and who may still be a part of such households in their adult lives.

I hope you find an uplifting, encouraging message in my story, which at last, I get to tell.

"Hope is the certainty that every question will be answered,
Every wrong will be made a right,
And every act of faithfulness will be rewarded."
– Anonymous

I have found a niche in my adult life. Don't we all, in the end, find our place?

I have always been a fighter, a giver. It felt good. Sometimes, I sit back looking at pictures of lovely young girls from my youth. The girls I grew up with, some friends of friends, distant family or mere acquaintances. Those lovely young girls led such easy and happy existences. I was never one of them. My feet hurt from the high heels I wore in my quest to be one of those lovely young girls. The "young" no longer applies, or matters, except perhaps to remind me that no matter how brave I was, in spite of my wide-open heart, the longing for what I had missed will never completely go away. Just looking at those pictures, I feel a pang of loss. These were girls who had caring, maternal mothers and present, protective fathers.

Time changes many things but it does not change our memories. I now overhear my eleven-year-old son announce to the nanny that he does not wish to go shopping at Kohl's anymore, only at the Holy Trinity of Abercrombie and Fitch, Aeropostale, and Hollister. The remark takes me back to my own childhood. Back to my observing from afar, already aware in elementary school that I did not fit in with the rest of the lovely young girls.

The Big House

I was only seven when I started to give the most absurd excuses as to why my father never came to the "Family Day Feast" that took place at my school every year but my mother simply said the same thing. My father was away at a medical conference.

My supposed best friend never stopped needling my unease, "How many medical conferences does your father have every month?" She added, "Are you sure your mother is telling the truth?"

I did not like having my mother's honesty challenged. My friend was always quick to add a gossipy flourish to any stories she deemed juicy enough to share, which were endless.

"You know, M's father is always taking off with his lover," she said in a rush. "X's mother is distraught because the father just bought the lover a brand new two-door Mercedes Benz and now X's mother is struggling to come up with money to pay for X's private gymnastics lessons."

As my friend prattled on, my heart raced so fast I thought she would see the pulse in my neck throb. The thought of my father taking off with a lover was an all too logical an explanation for his multiple absences. I was already a serious nail biter and had been one since age four. This new thought certainly wasn't going to relieve my anxiety.

We rarely ventured outside The Big House, the house that belonged to my grandparents, my mother's father and mother. The Big House stood on what used to be a cemetery for the slaves of a colonial nobleman. There were three floors, each with its own colonial-style Spanish terrace. On the ground floor an oversized bar, with colorful tiles of yellow and blue, adjoined the terrace. My grandparents had their bedroom on the third floor, which could be accessed only by a special lift my grandfather had ordered built after his open-heart surgery. My parents had their bedroom on the second floor, together with the bedrooms for the children: a very large corner one for my older sister, and two smaller ones that shared a bathroom for my little brother and me. There was also a guest room where my uncle, my mother's only brother, stayed when he visited. He had also grown up in The Big House, in that very room. He had wisely left The Big House to pursue a freer, lighter existence, away from the burdens that the house made us all ultimately carry. It's in the nature of every child to go off into the world and seek their own path. In his case, I think maybe it was more about survival.

My grandfather built the house in 1945, just after the war, one year before my mother was born. The house was full of secrets, full of ghosts. The neighbors claimed to frequently see a man, dressed in a coarse, white cotton shirt and trousers—what a slave would have worn one hundred and fifty years ago—walking down the street in front of The Big House. The children of the neighbors had tried to follow him, but as soon as he turned the corner of the Marques Del Toro Avenue, he disappeared, no doubt wandering after centuries-old unfinished affairs that were not for us to see.

My sister saw him once from up on the second-floor terrace, overlooking the main laundry room, where the clothes were hung to dry. She tells the story of how she saw a man dressed in white, barefoot, coming in from the street, walking along the open garage and making his way into the house. He opened the back door leading to the laundry room, only to never make it. Instead, at that exact moment, time and space became one. He crossed a portal linking present and past, vanishing from my sister's sight. It must have been the enactment of a never-ending errand; one he was to never quite finish. Who knows what that backdoor opened into, one hundred and fifty years ago, when the man had roamed the plantation in the flesh? It struck me as particularly sad, forever walking the same path and never reaching his destination, or worse still, being stuck in a role thrust upon him for eternity.

There were ghosts and there were secrets. My mother's hysterical, histrionic fits were covered up by her parents, her brother, and God bless them, the loyal servants. Even today I cannot say whether those episodes were psychotic in nature, or just a convenient outlet for an extremely selfish human being who had been spoiled all her life, a master at manipulation since infancy, as I've come to believe. The space between the walls of The Big House was charged with the anguish of her ever-present unhappiness. It was a different kind of haunting.

***

The Big House stood empty for many years. On January 23rd, 1958, Venezuela's dictatorship took a fall. My grandparents, my mother, and my uncle were forced to flee. They set up residence in Spain, our ancestral land. From there, my mother was shipped away to an all-girls boarding school in Switzerland run by French nuns. She stayed there for five years, after which she completed her education at Rosslyn House, a finishing school for girls in Surrey, England. My mother exhibited great intelligence and managed to be the recipient of numerous academic awards. She mastered the French language as if it were her own, developing an exquisite sensibility to delicate, soft and soothing poetry that contrasted with her mercurial temper. The years in Europe marked the beginning of a Golden Age of dinner parties and soirees that continued long after it became safe to return to Venezuela.

My father met my mother when he came home to his exiled parents in Spain, on holiday from the college in America where he was a student. My uncle had also enjoyed the privilege of a North American education, as was customary for affluent young men at the time but that is where the similarities ended. There could not have been two more different men. Very early in his life, my uncle was already old. My father always remained an adolescent, never quite reaching maturity. My parents married at the majestic San Fernando El Grande church in Madrid. They were painfully young and my mother's father tried to persuade her to break the engagement. She, in turn, threatened to elope. Thus, my parents embarked on a marriage that had been wrong, neither blessed nor welcome, from the very beginning.

***

School started at age four with prekindergarten. My grandfather's driver took me to the small, exclusive pre-elementary school every morning. There was never a sighting of my father or mother. Ever. As was her habit, mother did not wake up before noon. She was never ready to begin her day before two o'clock in the afternoon, as she would always have one of the maids bring her breakfast in bed. I happened to be in her room one morning, during the elementary school years (having fearfully interrupted her sacred sleep), telling her about some field trip with the school, when she began to grow impatient. Her breakfast had not arrived on time. In distress, she picked up the phone in the room and dialed the number that rang in the kitchen and alerted the servants to all her whims. Within minutes, an older maid dressed in black with a pristine white apron showed up carrying a perfectly polished silver tray that was used only for my mother's breakfast. It was Tomasa, the cook. She apologized for being late, explaining that Florinda, the younger maid who was in charge of breakfast in bed, had taken ill during the night. My mother could not have cared less.

"Mama, Florinda is sick! Mama, Florinda is going to die!" I cried, my voice breaking with the tears I was trying so hard to hold back. My mother said nothing. She stared straight ahead, at nothing in particular. Several minutes of an embarrassing (for me) silence went by.

"Anita, don't you worry," said Tomasa, using her pet name for me, a bit of affection I never saw from my mother. "Florinda has just a little cold." Tomasa smiled the saddest smile with her warm black eyes.

I loved Tomasa, our oldest and most skilled cook. She was a diminutive woman, standing, at most, four feet, ten inches, who arrived at the Big House when she was still a young girl, trying to escape the misery and the suffering that poor men and women from the Venezuelan countryside who were destined, one could say, by birthright to endure. It was here that she met her husband, Roso Cardozo Cardenas, whom she married while still a teenager. He was a brute of a man, an incorrigible alcoholic, violent and abusive, his anger stemming from the abuse he had suffered himself in the hands of a drunken father. Why must the kindest souls endure the most suffering?

"Anita, Baby Jesus will cure Florinda," she added. "I promise."

Rushing to Tomasa, I hugged her, putting my cheek next to hers, feeling the oil of her brown skin on my skin. "Be careful! I'm going to drop the tray for La Senora on the floor!"

All day long, Tomasa labored next to my grandmother, who was a splendid cook herself, and patiently learned all the recipes for the rich foods my grandmother wanted her to make. She baked a wonderful vanilla sponge cake and made impossibly sweet honey mango shakes for my brother and me. I loved Tomasa's son, Roso, too. In later years Roso would desperately try to change his given name to something he considered manlier. My brother and I affectionately called him Rosin. He was four years younger than me, a perfect playmate but an unlucky child whose mother would ultimately die in his arms when he was only ten, felled by an inoperable gastric tumor. Life brought us together and made us siblings through the tears of our grief.

Tomasa proceeded to lay down the breakfast tray. There were delicately scrambled fresh eggs, laid that morning by the hens in my grandfather's Gallinero or chicken pen; strong, aromatic coffee; orange juice; two lightly toasted slices of white bread; English butter and French strawberry preserves. Next to the orange juice stood a tall glass of water. My mother picked up the glass of water first to help her take her pills. She took as many as six different pills in the morning, just to even out her mood, something I couldn't quite understand at the time. I only understood that she hadn't look well but rather pale, thin, colorless and washed out, almost lost in the whitish beige background of sheets, blankets and bed covers. That morning, the only things that stood out in the pale sunlight of fading memory were the bright yellow of the orange juice on the tray, the red jar of French preserves, and Tomasa's black uniform.

After dressing with great care and attention to her clothes and makeup, my mother left the Big House. She never returned earlier than seven in the evening. There was always a hairdresser's appointment to go to or a shopping expedition planned. She would bring my brother and I a small toy or some crayons and coloring books she had picked up while out at the shops. Those small, almost daily gifts were the only tangible evidence of our mother's love for us. After the delivery of whatever small thing she had chosen to buy that day, she would spend a little time with us, always paying more attention to my brother.

My brother was a sweet boy, soft-spoken and meek, eighteen months younger than me. I was neither sweet, nor soft spoken, nor meek. My mother made sure I knew that. She made sure I knew I always appeared to be cross. Her special nickname for me was "Bull Face," because, as she explained to people, I always looked like an angry bull. My mother never even looked at my older sister, who was also sweet, soft-spoken, and meek. The only remarks my mother made about my sister were how she couldn't wait for my sister to stop growing so that she could have her nose fixed (apparently one needed to stop growing to have any kind of plastic surgery), and how dumb my sister was.

I always wondered why my mother didn't like my sister. It may have had to do with the fact that my sister was female. My mother told us both that she had only ever wanted to have boys, never girls: "I love men," she said on more than one occasion, "I have wonderful relationships with men. My relationship with my father and my son is heaven." There was never any mention of my father. My father was not worthy to be a part of her male relationship heaven.

So, while my mother slept her beauty sleep, the driver brought me to school. I was dropped off at seven-thirty in the morning. Two hours later, even though the session wouldn't end for another three hours, I would begin pestering my teacher to call my house to make sure that somebody would be there to pick me up when school was over. I never got over the lie my mother told the night before my first day of kindergarten. She had come into my room, all smiles and warmth. "Tomorrow I'm going to take you to a morning birthday party. Your nanny will be making your favorite snack, French bread and strawberry preserves, so you can take it with you." In her mind, this story fixed the problem of explaining the lunch box that I was going to have to take to school. The following morning, I was dropped off not at a birthday party, but a building with children and parents going every which way. I did not know where I was or why. I cried and trembled through what became my first fully conscious experience of abandonment but certainly not the last at the hands of my mother. The confusion and anguish are still fresh in my mind.

Late each afternoon, the adults gathered around the faux fireplace in the living room, amidst the golden rose tones of the baroque styled Louis XVI furniture that was fashionable at the time. The men held heavy crystal glasses filled with whisky, which they swirled in their hands, from time to time, the ice cubes clinking against the glass. The background burble of their conversation and laughter soothed my anxious little heart.

One such lazy summer afternoon, my aunts Esther, Beatriz, Thais, my great aunts Chela, Olga, and Esperanza, and their husbands, were gathered in the living room, with my parents and grandparents. It was still sunny, though late, the day refusing to die.

"Let's go downstairs to play on the terrace," I told my brother. We were in my mother's bedroom where boredom was beginning to set in.

"No! I want to stay here watching Batman and Robin," he said, eyes never leaving the screen. "You go. Besides, our mother said Tomasa could bring our pancakes here to her room and I am very hungry." We had pancakes for dinner two to three times a week.

My brother may have been sweet and meek but no soul ever had been able to force him to do something he didn't want to do. He was a master at passive resistance and by now I knew it was not in his plans to come down to the terrace to play with me that evening.

I ventured down alone. My eagerness to go outside subsided as I heard the familiar comforting noise of the adults in the living room, enthralled in their conversation. Sometimes these gatherings didn't end until after midnight, when all the whisky had been drunk and the clinking from the glasses had come to an end, as all the ice had melted. The ladies would then stand up to go to the bathroom, clutching their elegant bags as the men searched through the cabinets for one last measure of stupor.

I halted on the bottom step and stood there, listening, mesmerized. A strong, powerful male voice seemed to grow louder and closer to the staircase. Someone had stood up, paused for a moment, to leave their crystal glass on a side table, and fast approached. I ran to the formal dining room, directly opposite the stairs, and hid under the table. The dining room table sat sixteen people, but we children never sat there, as it was reserved for the adults. I safely hid under the heavy tablecloth, sitting on the floor, knees to chest.

The man with the loud voice crossed the corridor and made a left turn into my grandfather's office right next to my hiding place in the dining room. He turned the light on and mumbled something to himself. All of a sudden, I shivered at the possibility of getting caught hiding under the table by myself, without my brother. The man came out of my grandfather's office, turned the light off, his footsteps clunking on the marble as he slowly walked back to the living room where the other adults were. I exhaled, so relieved that I found the courage to leave my hiding place under the table and go to the wall that gave to the living room. I pressed my right ear against the wall, sensing the coolness of the bricks underneath the paint.

I did not recognize the voices anymore. My eyes were closed and my arms loose and comfortable on my lap when the lights in the room went on and the entire group of adults were standing in the dining room doorway, looking at me.

I could hear all of them, one by one: "What is she doing here?" "This is outrageous." "She has no manners." "The audacity of spying on us."

I stood up, covered my face with my hands, and ran towards the stairs. On the fifth step I choked back tears and gasped for breath. On the tenth a waterfall streamed down my cheeks and onto the sides of my neck. At the top of the stairs, I sobbed loudly, embarrassed, as my brother looked on. I went to my room and locked myself there for what seemed like hours. No one came to see me; no adults came to talk to me. I can't help but think that perhaps a sharp reprimand might have been better than obvious dismissal. I stayed alone, in my room, with only my shame for company.

***

Even at such a tender age I somehow sensed something was terribly wrong at The Big House. My mother and father did not want to leave its comfort and opulence. To this day, I don't even know if my father ever contributed to the upkeep of the house or towards the servants' wages, but I doubt it. My grandfather footed the bills while my grandmother oversaw the army of cooks and nannies and my mother slept her sacred sleep.

Beauty was the most important quality a person could have, according to my mother. That's why she fixated on "correcting" my poor sister's nose, which my sister had actually inherited from our mother herself. Even though neither my mother nor grandmother had discovered any major flaws in my person, I was already afraid. Afraid of not being beautiful. Not only had I been born of the wrong sex, but I was not sure if I was beautiful in the eyes of my family. My mother did comment on all of my friends' beauty: "Look! Did you see how gorgeous "Luisa" looks today?" "She is so pretty." "You should wear your hair like she does." And so on. The only thing I knew for sure was that I was smart. My mother said I was smart, a not so small compliment from a woman with so few to give.

Whatever my mother said stuck with me for life. I wish I could peel from my adult consciousness those judgments and pronouncements my mother made when I was in elementary school. Divesting my memory of her belittlements was practically impossible, as my mother was an icon of beauty and intelligence. Or so thought everybody else. Her criticism was harsh, sudden, unprovoked, severe. The hurtful phrases spurted out of her mouth like shots from a lethal gun. "Why do you bite your nails?" "Your hands are ugly." I wanted to cry. I raced upstairs to my room, to the solace of my white bedroom set, of my bookcases full of my favorite books. There were two beds in my room. One of the maids slept with me since I was terrified to sleep by myself.

My brother couldn't sleep alone either but my mother took him in to sleep with her in her room. Of course, my father was never there. In those days, my mother had gone back to the university to study languages. During that time, she constantly had female student friends stay overnight at the Big House, whenever there was a major examination the following day and particularly towards the end of the academic year as they were preparing their graduation thesis.

My mother never took me in to sleep in her room except once, when she had a fellow university student stay for the night. It was after dinnertime on one of those study nights that my mother approached me. "My friend is sleeping over because we haven't finished our thesis, which is due tomorrow, and we are going to get up at 4 AM tomorrow morning to finish it. She will be sleeping in your room so you can come and sleep with me for tonight." I could barely hide my excitement: "Yes, Mama! Thank you, Mama!" I so wanted to be loved by her, to be praised by her, to be spoilt by her.

My mother was so very charming and sophisticated in front of her friends and anyone who visited The Big House. Unforgettable. Thoughtful. Kind. She made us kneel down to apologize to the maids if we were inappropriate or rude. My cousins adored her and sang her praises. My friends thought she was so pretty and smart; everyone admired her Audrey Hepburnesque physique and the accompanying refinement. She had very large reddish-brown eyes, and she knew how to highlight their striking effect with exactly the right shades of eye makeup. Whether she wore trousers, a dress or a skirt, her shoes and handbags as well as her accessories, which included real jewelry, were carefully chosen for a perfect match. Every time.

She was always ready to please. "I am off to the salon," she announced in her sweet, good-mood voice as she paraded along the kitchen on the way to the car. Everybody stopped what they were doing to watch her go by. Tomasa looked up from the bowl and the mixing spoon: "La Senora looks so elegant this afternoon. Enjoy your time at the salon, Senora." I glanced up from my notebook and my pencils, my grandmother from her bowl of pudding. We said nothing as Her Majesty went by.

My brother was my best friend. We took the beatings together. While our mother's verbal tirades were brutal, the physical abuse was just as savage. Yet, my older sister was beaten far more than we were. My mother bought a special leather whip in Paris. I did not know if the story my mother told was true, but she said it had come highly recommended as an efficient correctional instrument. All I knew is that my mother made my sister bleed with this whip. Bleed from her scalp, her arms, her legs. My sister accepted the abuse like a lamb. When my mother came near my brother and me with the whip, we ran away or hid under the bed, or simply stayed on the floor, curled up together in a ball as tightly as possible. Not my sister. She took it standing up. She cried, loudly, and covered her face with her hands, but she didn't run, didn't once try to escape my mother's wrath. As time has gone on, I look back and think it may have been a passive rebellion on my sister's part, a refusal to bow to the whim of her tormentor and retain the only measure of control she could have in that situation. She couldn't control the beatings, but she could her response.

We were never sure where our mother's terrible wrath came from, at least not then. We suffered her anger in the ignorance and innocence of childhood. We suffered her lack of patience, her irritability. Her inconsistency. We swallowed her detachment, choking on her never-ending criticism, her cruelty and her judgments. To some extent, my grandmother made up for my mother's cruelty. She never raised a hand to us. She even drove us to school for a while. Rising early, she made sure that the maids prepared our breakfast. She took us to the beach club on weekends, to church on Sundays, and on road trips around the country during school holidays. She supervised our homework, made us practice division and multiplication tables with her in the car. In spite of the blood tie, my grandmother's ways and style contrasted deeply with my mother's.

My grandmother was plagued all her life by a tendency to gain weight. Even my brother and I couldn't help but notice the plumpness of her body, its slowly expanding roundness. She was a pretty woman too, but not in the slim Audrey Hepburn way. Definitely not. Where my mother was sharp, my grandmother was soft in all manner of literal and figurative ways. God bless my grandmother, because she was there to support us in childhood. From my grandmother, I received the closest thing that I would ever experience to unconditional love, to the maternal love our mother denied us. Even later, when my grandmother, in her old age, became coarse and hurtful in her treatment of me, I remained grateful for the love and care she had once bestowed.

In addition to my grandmother, each of us children were assigned a nanny. My nanny fixed me small bites in the afternoons, cleaned my room and washed my clothes. She was my companion, my friend, and I adored her. These were the pillars of support, guidance and friendship of my young life. Simple acts of kindness or soft words where harsh ones were usually spoken are indelibly tattooed on the heart of a child and echo in remembrance in adulthood.

Tragedy

My father was a distant figure. He was tall and handsome, and bore a distinguished surname, hailing from a prominent family whose origins had been meticulously traced back by my grandfather to the ancient city of Oyarzun, in the province of Guipuzcoa, in the Spanish Basque Country. Undoubtedly influenced by the enormous success of The Royal Guipuzcoan Company of Caracas, a Basque company formed by a group of wealthy Guipuzcoans in 1728, the first Michelena arriving in Venezuela, Santiago Jose Ignacio de Michelena, was born in Oyarzun on July 25th, 1766. The records state he married Maria Teresa Rojas, a native of Venezuela in December of 1790. Their son, Santos Michelena, born in Maracay in 1797, would eventually become vice-president of Venezuela and a leading political figure, serving, additionally, as Head of the Ministry of Finance. He was my grandfather's great-great grandfather. Fearless explorers, the Basques were not only skilled navigators and engineers, but clever negotiators, ambitious entrepreneurs, and original thinkers. It was always a matter of pride that The Father of Latin American Independence, Simon Bolivar, a member of the Masonic Lodge, was also born in Caracas in 1783 to a Basque family who had grown very wealthy in South America.

One early September morning, when I was six years old and before the new school year had started, my mother miraculously and unexpectedly got herself ready before noon. She packed all her children in the latest model luxury car, given by my doting grandfather for her birthday that year. On the way, she told us we were going on a surprise visit to the Operating Room to see my father. My father came out from the shiny metallic double doors that bore, in oversized capital letters, the words "RESTRICTED

ACCESS". He looked gigantic, taller than I remembered. He was wearing green scrubs that brought out his leafy green eyes. On his head was a surgical hat, also green, and a white mask over his nose and mouth that he quickly pulled off with his gloved hands. It was very cold in the hospital corridor that morning. He saw us, and stopped, considering for a moment before approaching. No smile adorned his face and he didn't welcome the intrusion of his family into the sanctum of his professional world.

"Hello," he said to my mother, gazing at the wall behind her.

"Hello," she replied, facing him, staring at him in the eye, her face frozen.

He said nothing, letting out a sigh instead.

"You should be grateful I brought you the children this morning."

"Thank you," he said without interest. There was no bite in his words, he simply remained unaffected. Cold.

This vision of my father, and perhaps of the power I may have sensed he had over my scorned mother, gave me the sudden desire for authority and unrestricted access that, in my young mind, that pair of green scrubs gave him. I, too, wished to be anointed with scrubs, a surgical mask, and gloves.

My parents murmured to one another with mounting intensity, their voices descending into fierce whispers. I could not make out their words, but I sensed the conversation revolved around us, the children. He took her arm to lead her away from the nurses' station, and out of earshot of his colleagues, but she snatched her arm from his grasp, marching back to where we stood, shy and uncomfortable. Whatever my mother's aim, it had evidently not succeeded. She shooed us before her like baby chickens.

"Father," said my brother, looking over his shoulder, "I want to stay with my father."

She took him by the wrist and forced him forward. We all went along with her. There was no choice.

Yet this became one of the happiest moments of my entire childhood, a touchstone I returned to almost daily in my mind. It was the day I conceived the idea of becoming, like my father, an anesthesiologist.

I have no recollection of ever having a conversation with my father before he left The Big House four years later, the day my mother, the uncertain creature, lost whatever elegance she carried within. I was in my burgundy school uniform, sitting on the Persian carpet in my parents' bedroom, watching TV, which sometimes our mother would let us do. I smelled the sweat of the long school day in my uniform, feeling a little uncomfortable yet too lazy to change. There was loud knocking on the door. "I need to get my things." I recognized my father's voice. My mother, I noticed then, was emptying out his closet into black garbage bags.

She moved in a trance, talking to herself, exaggerated in all her movements. It was as if her soul was being exorcised from her body through her limbs and she had the look of a mad woman. The empty pupils of her gaze were terrifying. My father stood outside when my mother finally opened the door. She threw the garbage bags at him, full of his suits, ties, socks, shoes. And then she threw herself at him, screaming, slapping his face left and right, beating on his chest. Much like my sister, he said absolutely nothing in the face of her wrath, made no move to stop or evade her blows. I remained on the Persian carpet, transfixed by the spectacle. I wanted to get her off him but I couldn't move, my fear and confusion paralyzing.

At last my mother gave up, exhausted. She could do him no real hurt. She was too small and he was too large. Rounding on me, she screamed at the top of her voice: "You, get out of here. Now! Get out!"

Quickly and silently I left the room and my father departed our lives. I wanted to save him, to shield him from the devastating spectacle of her rage. I searched, in vain, inside my heart for the strength to protect him; only to realize I did not even know him. The man who walked out the door that day was as much a stranger to me as I must have been to him.

I stood in the corridor, outside my mother's room.

"Ana, Ana," a soft musical voice hailed from the end of the corridor. "Come here."

My sister signaled with both hands. She was standing under her doorway, in the corner room, her room. Her long brown hair, which she had let loose, framed her aqua eyes. Her gesturing was so intense I thought her eyes were going to pop out of her skull. I hurried along the long corridor. A door opened behind me, quickly, frantically. My sister disappeared into her room. I did not turn to look, but I knew I wasn't the only one in the corridor anymore. There was heavy breathing behind me.

Almost at my sister's room I turned around and took one quick look behind me. It was my mother, walking fast, taking short, very quick steps. I screamed with all my might, crossed the threshold of my sister's room and slammed the door shut. My sister hugged me as I was trying to catch my breath. There were three hard knocks at the door—Bang! Bang! Bang—and one single command: "Open!" My sister started laughing, something she did when she was emotionally overwhelmed. We locked ourselves in her bathroom, which happened to be side by side with my parents' bathroom. The knocking persisted. I was laughing too, so hard that tears were coming out of my eyes. It was a mixture of fear, awe, and stress.

It was then that my sister, holding my arms and looking into my eyes, asked. "Do you know what is going on?"

Before I could answer when her demeanor suddenly changed. She had a somber look about her.

"All night long I heard their arguing and screaming from the bathroom window. Father is leaving Mother for another woman, a patient at the clinic." Motionless, I sat in shock. Afraid. "It is not his first affair," my sister added.

"What's going to happen to us?" I said.

Outside, the angry banging came on the door once more.

"I don't know, Ana," my sister said. "I don't know."

***

Not long after my father left, my mother, my grandmother, and several great aunts, sisters of my grandmother, started the rumors. They whispered tales of how my father was being sued at both private clinics where he practiced as an anesthesiologist; of how he was an alcoholic and resorted to using drugs to manage the hangovers and withdrawals so that he would be able to go into the operating room in the mornings. The rumors didn't stop at fabricated addictions. My great aunts wove a frightening tale of how my father's lover, an obscure, middle-aged Polish woman, a lawyer by trade, had become well-versed in witchcraft and the practice of Voodoo. She was apparently putting all her effort and money into the formulation and application of "dark spells" to render my father helpless at her feet. The goodwill of my mother, my sister, my brother and I had not been powerful enough to stop the European witch's demonic machinations. The rumormongering had no effect. My father did not return, and his practice continued to be a success.

My birthday brought me the joy of a beautiful pet rabbit and the promise of being allowed to wear whatever I found in a small jewelry gift box that my father sent to the house that day. Of course, I could only wear it after it had been cleansed and made pure of all evil purposes and intentions by Holy Water, which my grandparents had bought on one of their trips to the

Holy Land. In the end, my mother did not even let me see the gift, let alone wear it.

Instead, that night, my mother sat all of us children down.

"Now that your father has abandoned you," she declared, "we are alone in the world."

We sat, the three of us, on a couch, facing my mother. Her eyes flashed with anger and resentment, her posture stiff with accusation. I hated those words—"Your father abandoned you!"—And their implication that somehow we had not been good enough children to make our father want to stay with us.

"Don't say that!" I felt an unaccustomed ferocity. "Don't you use those words when you refer to father. You say, 'My husband who abandoned me.'"

Taken aback, my mother said, "What do you know of it?"

"I know it was you who chose him as your husband and the father of your children," I said. "It was you who decided to bear more children even though you hated being a mother from the day my sister was born."

My mother stared coldly. Next to me, my brother sat rigid, and I could feel, on the other side, my sister trembling, but I was too angry for fear. Lifting my chin, I met her eyes. After all, she had already admitted, as though it were nothing, that she had borne three children only because it was fashionable to do so in the socialite world she inhabited. Unwanted. Unloved. Ideas planted at such a young age would blossom into a lifetime of doubt and insecurity. How could they not?

My mother warned us that, with my father gone, we faced financial difficulties. As children, we did not know what this meant, and we were terrified.

"Are we poor?" I asked. "How are we to pay for school, or food, or medicine when we fall ill?"

"I don't know," she replied.

Casting a final look of contempt at me, she turned and swept out of the parlor and up the stairs toward her room.

The moment I heard her answer was the very moment something erupted from deep inside of me and surrounded me completely. The blood in my limbs froze. From that moment forward, my life was governed by nuances of anxiety, vigilance, hyper alertness. Like many children from broken homes, I assumed responsibility for everyone around me, including the adults.

***

In spite of the tumultuous nature of our household, many of my happiest memories revolve around Christmas. My grandmother made sure the strongest family holiday traditions were observed at the Big House. Always at least seven feet tall, the Christmas tree was decorated with the most colorful, shiny ornaments that I would ever encounter. Its delicious scent of fresh pine permeated the whole house. The Christmas tree lights were kept on day and night. It was the same with the lights on the Nativity scene, a scene crafted to include mountains made of sackcloth, streams of blue cellophane paper, the shiniest Star of Bethlehem, and more than thirty figurines. My brother and I spent hours looking at it, telling each other stories about which shepherd would arrive at the manger first, and of the order in which the Magi would present their gifts.

All throughout the Christmas season, Tomasa busied herself in the kitchen, roasting turkey, pheasant, special ham and chestnut pudding. Wild rice steamed to perfection, glorious hen meat, salad, and of course the ubiquitous tamal, were also part of her repertoire. Every two or three days, she put out her Christmas sugar cookies for us. My brother and I dipped them in our milk. We counted down the days until Christmas Eve, when the final tally of the gifts under the tree took place. My mother and her socialite friends always made sure there were plenty. One year I had twenty-seven presents under the tree.

One Christmas Eve loud footsteps sounded on the second-floor Spanish terrace. It was late, almost midnight. My brother and I could barely contain our excitement. We made bets on who would get the most toys (winner) and who the most clothes (loser, obviously). There had already been a lot of commotion around the house that evening, as was usual for the occasion, when suddenly, my uncle appeared in the parlor where the Christmas tree stood. He carried a pistol in his right hand. Without saying hello or goodbye, he rushed through the room and out the door that gave on to the patio, in the back. It was an alarming sight that chilled the Christmas cheer at a blow. All the servants gathered in the room, with worried faces. The nannies held our hands.

We heard my uncle fire several shots, presumably into the air. He raced up the outdoor stairs that led to the second floor. I could not envision my uncle shooting at a human being. Fifteen minutes later, he came down.

"I managed to scare and chase the thief away," he said. His breathing came short and his hands trembled. Setting the pistol carefully on a high shelf, he lowered himself onto a couch, his eyes staring fixedly at something not inside the room. Coming to himself, he added, "We are safe now."

"I wish you had killed him!" declared one of the younger maids.

"No, no," said my uncle. "He is an unfortunate. He must be desperate, to be out thieving on this of all nights, and in a house ablaze with lights! It is the thought that I might have had to shoot that man that makes me tremble."

My mother laughed musically, in a voice that came to her in parties and other social situations.

"You are scaring the children with these absurdities," she said. Turning to us, she added, "Do not be afraid. The noises on the second floor were made by the hooves of Santa's reindeer as the sleigh landed on the terrace."

My brother and I were delighted with this explanation, and we believed her without question. It was the only time my mother was ever protective of our innocence.

**

My brother and I were very close as we grew up, joined by an invisible thread. Barely a year older, I took it upon myself to tutor him with his schoolwork. I wanted him to do well. Many years later he credited me with having planted the seed for learning, and most importantly, for doing well in life, as he put it. It was as if we both thought that doing well at school would buy us the love and acceptance we unconsciously sought to receive at The Big House.

My sister, by contrast, was not a good student. She struggled with schoolwork, constantly requiring the presence of private and expensive tutors to assure her a passing grade. My sister loved music, painting and drawing. She was an attractive girl with a relaxed, yet bubbly personality and the lightest approach to life. She was a fun girl, a beach going, party loving girl. Her beautiful spirit was never fully appreciated at The Big House. At first, I did well at school out of fear of being rejected at home if I did poorly. But then, I really started to enjoy the process of learning. All those years of hard study fostered the mental discipline and the work ethic that I put to good use in my adult life.

There was a cousin who visited often, the son of one of my grandmother's sisters. Frederic was studying to be a lawyer and, for some reason, loved spending time with my brother and me. We were seven and eight. In my grandfather's library, Frederic randomly picked a character from world history. We had to research the life of this personage and write out the information in the form of an essay he would afterwards grade us on. As a result of this game, we knew about Machiavelli's Prince and the

Ninety-five Theses that Martin Luther nailed to the door of Wittenberg Castle church over four centuries ago. My fascination for gathering and later recalling what some would refer to as "useless information" had been kindled. Even after Frederic departed, I often stayed in my grandfather's library, researching and studying.

An intellectual connection is not all that I shared with my brother. We also had a strong emotional bond. Whatever was done onto him I felt was equally done onto me. Once, after racing each other on the patio, he fell and skinned his knee. The nannies alerted my mother, who immediately fetched the bottle of antiseptic my brother and I feared. My brother was sitting on top of a large rock that lay in one of the corners of the patio. When I saw my mother. I ran to her, grabbing her by the thighs, begging her not to use the antiseptic on my brother's bleeding knee. She pulled me away and held me in front of her, while she explained to me that the disinfection of my brother's wound was mandatory and that my apprehension was uncalled for, unacceptable. Thinking only of the pain soon to be imposed upon my brother's raw knee, I persisted. "This girl is unbelievable! Lord!" she cried. "What have I done wrong to deserve her!"

She proceeded to pour the strong-smelling liquid on a cotton swab, at which point I fainted at my brother's feet. My mother later recounted the story to her friends, laughing. It was a heartbreaking lesson to find mockery where compassion should live, and the need to keep my feelings hidden blossomed from that day forward.

It's easy to think that the absence of my father may have tempered my mother's fire, but there was no diminishing her inferno. Even with this new vacuum in our family, it felt as if nothing had changed, which leads me to think that my father had never really been present at all. This new reality was the physical manifestation of what had been emotionally true since I was born.

Bittersweet

During the summer holidays, my grandmother took us to the beach club where we rented an apartment for what felt like an entire lifetime to us, two months. The nannies packed our bags the night before as my brother and I planned future games and activities for the beach and the pool. The trip, normally less than one hour by car, took almost two, as my grandmother not only drove the speed limit but also stopped twice on the way for "cocadas" (coconut milk shakes) and "cazon" (baby shark) empanadas.

Those were the best sixty days of the year. All day long, my brother and I explored the club, accompanied by one of the nannies. There was a mirror pool with transparent glass walls, in front of which the nanny sat and watched us swim laps and play our games. The nannies were not allowed in the pool. There was also the "serpent" pool, built in the shape of a snake, with secret turns and hidden underwater passages. And lastly, there was the Olympic pool, with a four-story-high diving platform. My brother and I avoided the Olympic pool after one of the neighbor's children, five-year-old Menachem, drowned in it. Our favorite spots at the club were the serpent pool and, of course, the beach.

The beach was long, broad, wide, with fat waves of crystalline bluish green topped by white froth. My mother said that seawater was high in iodine, a natural disinfectant for scrapes and wounds. We checked each other for skinned knees and elbows before braving the water, courageously taking the sting of the salt in the wounds as the waves lifted us high in the air.

On the club wharves, my brother and I became avid fishermen, talking for hours as we waited for the fish to bite.

"Do you think they will be taking us to see Mickey Mouse this year?" my brother asked, letting out a long sigh.

"Our grades are excellent," slipped out of my mouth, unexpectedly, "that's the only thing that matters to them."

"Are you saying that if we had awful grades, they would never take us to Disney World?" he replied, his seven year old voice breaking.

"Probably not." I answered absentmindedly, as the fish were pulling on the bait at the end of my rod. "But don't you worry about it. I will convince Grandmother to take us. I think she loves us a little more than the other adults and she will give in."

Back in the apartment, the nanny cleaned whatever we caught that day, tossing the small, whitish pieces in the sizzling oil of a frying pan. There were movies to watch at the open theatre, games of bowling and mini golf championships. During the two summer months at the beach club, we did not miss my mother or my father, not even for a moment.

***

Things had continued to spiral for my mother. After my father left the Big House, she telephoned the mother of one of my schoolmates at the Catholic academy and told her everything. My parents' separation became public knowledge. I grew anxious as September and the new school year approached, fearful of the judgment I was sure would come my way.

Mercifully, no one at my school knew about an incident at the beach club when my mother had once tried to kill my father. I am still not sure how the gossip was contained. While my brother and I were at the beach club for a weekend, we overheard some adults talking about a crazy woman, up in one of the beach apartments, who had fired a gun at her husband because she had discovered he was having an affair. The bullet missed. She chased her husband out of the apartment and down the corridor in her nightgown, waving the pistol and yelling insults and profanities. I felt a tiny piercing of anxiety, listening to this, but quickly dismissed it. One day, I was immersed in a book in my grandfather's library and apparently invisible to my mother, who walked in unexpectedly and picked up the phone to dial one of her friends.

"Yes, it was me," she said. "I shot at that son of a bitch. I caught him lying again. I caught him on the phone with her as he promised her the moon and the stars and a brand new car if she would wait for him to divorce me."

She listened for a moment, then laughed.

"No, no," she said. "My only regret is that I didn't kill him."

Then, I knew. The crazy woman at the club had been my mother. Even our summer respite had now been tainted by my mother.

After my father's departure, an ocean of immorality and chaos swallowed us all. My mother cried and wailed all day, like a soul in purgatory, atoning for unimaginable sins. She completely exchanged the daytime for the nighttime, asleep all day, awake all night. We almost never saw her. She looked distraught, even sadder than when my grandfather had died, four years earlier.

I barely remember my grandfather but had always heard he was a noble, generous man. In addition to The Big House, my grandfather owned a vacation house in the countryside. Every weekend, my grandparents went to the country home or stayed at one of the haciendas that belonged to the main investor at the firm where my grandfather worked. They had taken me to the country house once or twice. My grandfather let me ride his horse, with him riding behind me. I was five years old and it was a wonderful feeling, sitting high on the horse, secure and proud of my grandfather.

That night, by mistake, I opened the bathroom door in the flat where we were staying. My grandfather stood in front of the sink, shaving. I couldn't help but notice the protruding scar down the middle of his chest, where Dr. Denton Cooley in Texas, had cut open his sternum and had given him a brand new heart valve. It was the first time I was aware of my grandfather being a sick man. He had suffered rheumatic fever as a child, and the unforgiving streptococcus had done away with his aortic valve. In 1976, a year after my grandfather's heart operation, Dr. Cooley sent an urgent telegram, making all his patients around the world aware that the prosthetic valve he had used on them was defective and was causing emboli and strokes. The recommendation had been to undergo a second open-heart procedure to replace the faulty valve. For reasons of his own, my grandfather refused to undergo another major surgery, even though he had been only sixty-six years old at the time. Three months after the Texas telegram, he suffered the disabling stroke that would ultimately lead to his death.

The weeks leading up to the stroke must have been very difficult for him. He was likely plagued by fear and anxiety over what would happen to all of us at The Big House if he were to die. In addition to such ominous preoccupation, he had practically lost sight in one of his eyes. This was extremely worrisome for him, for obvious and not so obvious reasons. While tending to his doves on the patio, he was briefly distracted by one of the doves in the cage when a long, thin branch from his favorite tree, a lemon tree, scratched his cornea.

Florinda, the maid who later told me the story, had her back to my grandfather, but could see his form out of the corner of her eye. Suddenly he reached a hand to his face. He lost his balance, leaning on the dovecote for support. My mother, sitting in the garden, saw him, too.

"Papa! Papaito!"

She rose from her chair, her poetry book falling open on the patio, as she ran to him.

"Papa, what is it?"

My grandfather said he had injured his eye and asked for my uncle to be summoned.

I asked Florinda if my mother was crying. "Your mother was crying, yes," she said. "But remember, it takes very little to bring her to tears."

My uncle took my grandfather to the ophthalmologist, who tried all sorts of treatments and measures to promote healing, to no avail. The scratch became a chronic sore that would not heal.

During the last visit to the ophthalmologist, on being told that the sore would never heal, my uncle told my mother and all of us children that my grandfather suddenly remembered an event from thirty-five years earlier. He had been twenty-six years old and held a post dealing with international customs. Some unruly sailors had stolen several boxes of Cuban cigars from an elderly, dark-skinned woman. My grandfather supervised the successful confiscation of the cigars from the sailors and their brisk return to their rightful owner. That was how she earned a living, by selling cigars and whisky in the black market. She appeared at my grandfather's office just before lunchtime to thank him for the recovered cigars. She said she was very poor and unable to read or write but wanted to give him a gift as a token of her gratitude. She was going to see the future for him.

"Catire," she affectionately called him, meaning fair-skinned one in Spanish, "You are a good man. You are going to be very successful in life. You will cross a big body of water, live abroad and continue to be successful. Regretfully though, I am seeing that you want me to tell you about the time of your death. I cannot reveal that to you, Catire. They don't let us. I will only tell you that close to the time of your death, you will be blind in one eye."

My grandfather's mood darkened at the memory of the prediction of long ago that, almost in its entirety, had already taken place: his successful business, his exile in Spain. And now, this: the chronic eye infection that would never heal. He knew his time was near.

Coincidence? Superstition? Wild guess? How could an analphabet woman have known all that, so many years ago, in the Venezuelan countryside?

For this, I still have no answer.

During the two weeks following his stroke, my grandfather was barely conscious, yet still alive. He was on the respirator and cried a lot whenever he saw his two children, my uncle and my mother, at his side. His funeral took place in November, on a gray, overcast day with light yet persistent rain. Family and friends gathered to bid their last goodbyes. What no one had expected was the arrival of busloads of people at the burial site. Young and old, women and men, people unknown to the family. They came in gratitude to pay their respects. Gratitude for an elderly woman's hospital bills that my grandfather had taken care of. For the studies at the university of someone's son that my grandfather had paid for. And much more. Neither my grandmother, my uncle, nor my mother had known of my grandfather's secret acts of kindness. The idea that such a kind and giving man had fathered my mother was almost unbelievable. He loved well.

My grandmother was the love of his life. She was much younger than my grandfather, an attractive, feisty woman, an orderly homemaker and an excellent cook. She loved travelling and always did it in style. Both my grandparents appreciated the good things in life, spring travel in the North of Africa, winter sleigh rides in Finland, exquisite white wine delivered to the house directly from Germany. Life always seemed to unfold in exciting, vibrant ways for them.

I can never forget the time my grandmother took me to the pediatrician to get a prediction of my final adult height by means of an X-ray of my hand. I was nine years old and one of the shortest in the class at school. Being short herself, she was obsessed with my future height. Despite her own good fortune, she believed only tall women had a chance of getting worthy, handsome men in life. The X-ray of my hand predicted a final height of only five foot and two inches. For the first three days after the visit to the pediatrician, she was in denial. Since my father stood six feet three inches, and since I looked like my father, she convinced herself that the X-ray prediction had to be wrong. A week later, she changed her mind and made an appointment at the endocrinologist and arranged for me to receive growth hormone injections. My mother, being short and beautiful herself, put an end to the treatment before it could begin. In the end, much to my own dismay, the prediction turned out to be painfully accurate yet it never interfered with any of the goals I set myself to attain over the years: my mother, for once, had been right.

My grandmother, very much in the same spirit of her generous husband, believed her grandchildren should see the world. She had always wanted for us to spend a year studying abroad. For my sister, she chose a Catholic, all-girls school run by Irish nuns thirty minutes by train south of London. My sister was fourteen years old at the time and, of course, didn't want to go. There had always been friction between my sister and my grandmother, who was critical of her happy-go-lucky ways. Yet, my sister ended up loving her year abroad and making friends with girls from all over the world. Many of her classmates were the children of English diplomats, who chose to send their daughters to boarding school in England rather than taking them abroad, thus securing their well-rounded English education.

In view of my parents' imminent divorce, the timetable for my brother and me to study in England was accelerated. We left The Big House for England at the end of the school year. I had just turned eleven. My mother came with us on account of our tender years. She rented a house in the same town where my school was, and supposedly pursued studies in English literature at the University of London. But who knows how she actually spent her time? I seldom saw her. Sometimes, on Mondays, she would visit with the nuns during schoolwork hours and drop off a loaf of lemon cake from Waitrose for me to snack on during the week. The fact that she would only visit during schoolwork hours and never when I was available to see her did not end up mattering in the end, as I loved that lemon cake. My mouth turns to water at the thought of it to this day.

Oddly, since he was the favorite, my brother saw our mother even less. He was ensconced in a boarding school for boys fifty minutes away from the house where my mother lived. For him, the visits were restricted to festive days and half-term holidays. My arrangement suited me. I was happy to be by myself, reading, learning about the world. Nobody knew me. Nobody knew my parents were divorced. It was a fresh, liberating start for me and I thrived academically. I mastered the English language quickly and became acquainted with the French language too, while always placing in the top group for math and science. I thoroughly enjoyed learning Latin and even considered taking up another foreign language, German.

I did not miss my mother. When I thought of her at all, it was to brood over her betrayals. At the age of eleven, I had lost much of my faith in her. I thought her weak, incapable, untrustworthy. I could not bring myself to miss the erratic woman or the chaos often left in her wake. My brother felt differently. He endured a stern priest for a headmaster and the strictest of teachers, all male. In fact, there was not a single female teacher in the entire school. His adjustment to this new system was very difficult. He had a special connection with my mother that would make his stay at the boarding school all the harder. This connection would end up adding much pain to his life over the years. I was already forming the decision not to pay the steep price that a close connection with my mother commanded. I sensed, even if I did not quite know it consciously, that I was better off without her.

The days grew shorter as winter set in. The hundred-year-old convent housed boarders from all over the world. There were girls from Spain, Belgium, Holland, Australia, India, Singapore, Malaysia, Hong Kong, Korea. Even Mauritius had its representation at the school. We sat at hundred-year-old desks and wrote with old-fashioned fountain pens that, if we were not careful, made a mess of the paper and of our fingers. Perhaps because we were from differing nationalities and cultures, social life at the convent was less cliquish than what I knew from home, with less malicious gossip. I enjoyed talking with the older girls and learning what life was like in their country of origin. I became quite close to one of the Asian girls, Corinne Khor, a charming, beautiful girl from Korea. She was sixteen, five years my senior, when our short friendship commenced. We always sat together in the refectory, discussing whichever books we happened to be reading at the moment, over cold slices of white bread and strawberry marmalade. Apparently, the Sisters did not believe in toast for breakfast.

Sometime during the winter term, Corinne took ill. She no longer made appearances at the refectory, or at prep time, when we would all sit together to do schoolwork. She even stopped coming for tea and biscuits at four-fifteen in the afternoon, a ritual I cherished and which she never missed. I ventured into the sixth form dormitory looking for her, only to learn she had been moved to the infirmary, a smallish, poorly lit room in the Sisters' private quarters. I quickly walked the stairs down to find my way there.

Corinne was lying on a bed, looking sickly and feverish. She had a severe case of jaundice; her skin had taken on a bright yellow hue. She was seriously ill, with an acute case of hepatitis. I held her hand and attempted to comfort her, but she was too feverish to speak coherently. Presumably, she had caught it over the winter holidays, when she had last travelled to South America where her father was stationed as the South Korean ambassador to Brazil. Either the nuns failed to gauge the severity of Corinne's illness, or the course of her ailment had been truly sudden.

Corinne Khor died that winter, in the infirmary at the convent, without her parents. I was inconsolable, unable to process her youth, her illness, the absence of her family, and her sudden, unexpected death. A few days later, her parents appeared sobbing, hugging each other. On the last day of the last month of that dreadful year, Corinne made her final journey home to South Korea, with her mother at her side. We planted a white flowering bush by the entrance of the school, IN MEMORIAM. In memoriam of a dead friend. In the years to come, I would often think about Corinne, and would be forever taken by her kindness and willingness to befriend an obscure eleven-year-old girl from South America. Corinne had been a lighthouse for me, shining its light in the middle of the dark storm of my young life, reminding me of the kindness and goodwill of humanity. She had not only been a role model but a friend. Corinne possessed a rare combination of traits: she commanded my respect and admiration for her composure and poise while at the same time, her soft, non-judgmental ways inspired enough trust to peel off the impenetrable layers of stoicism that I, by necessity, had placed over my emotional persona in order to shield myself from further criticism and ridicule .Corinne always listened with an intent ear; always paid attention to what I had to say. She smiled often and even had the sisters give us apricot pie (my favorite) for my birthday. When she was no longer there, the heavy layers of my armor were irreversibly laid back on. The other students who were my age could not begin to understand why I was so affected by her death or why I had befriended an older girl in the first place and every explanation proved to be beyond their ability to emotionally process the reasons behind my devastation. Corinne possessed emotional control yet she inspired trust; two of the traits that a child looks for in the adults in her life... by being older than me, yet completely approachable, Corinne had allowed me to, ever fleetingly, feel watched and cared for, perhaps, in the foreign environment of a boarding school, even feel protected. I tried to convey my feelings of loss to my mother who, morbidly, seemed more interested in the details of Corinne's illness and death: "How did she look when she died? she asked. "How old are her parents?" she insisted. "Did her mother cry a lot when she saw her?" At that moment I realized there was no solace to be found in my mother to lessen the pain of my loss.

It struck me as so unfair that my life continued on, with the same constant push and pull with my mother, while hers had been so tragically cut short but even in my youth I was quickly learning that life could be hugely unfair.

In the time that followed, while I mourned the loss of Corrine, life quickly returned to the mundane. In spite of the new excitements of a young girl in a new country and a whole new social group, I remained fearful and withdrawn. A new level of anxiety had set in; a paralyzing sense of being utterly afraid of life and terrified of all the possible ways in which all manner of things could go wrong. In trying to process the tragedy of Corinne's unexpected death on my own, I almost lost all sense of faith in life: almost all sense of hope.

Three months before my twelfth birthday, the Sisters suggested I should get my eyesight checked. They told my mother I squinted in class and was always requesting to sit at the very front. It turned out I was extremely nearsighted: blind as a mole, perhaps even a bat. My mother was mortified by the news. "We must get you fitted for contact lenses right away," she insisted.

Not understanding what the fuss was about, I suggested shopping for a pair of eyeglasses. "Absolutely not! You will look very ugly in them. We have to get you the contact lenses."

I became aware of something new then, though I did not fully understand it all at once. The sting of my mother's cruelty in using the word "ugly" ignited in me a compassion for others, especially children. No child becomes ugly because they wear glasses. No child should be told they are ugly. Not by their mother. Not to their faces. Not behind their backs. I knew there was something wrong in the cavalier way my mother tossed the word around, frequently in the direction of her youngest daughter, but many years would pass before I pieced all the moral, ethical, and psychological bits together. My mother's casual cruelty did have one salutary effect. In my zeal to be as little like her as possible, it ignited in me a compassion for others, especially the less fortunate, those who, with complete unfairness, people like my mother would condemn as "ugly."

Given her low opinion of my physical attractiveness, my mother would have been shocked at the amount of unexpected attention I began receiving from the opposite sex. On several occasions, my mother sent me on family trips that my brother's school organized. I also attended school dances, which were charmingly awkward, as they tend to be at that in-between stage of life. It was at one of those school dances, near the beginning of the year, that the very first boy of my life approached me. All the other girls thought he was the most handsome second former in the whole county of Guildford. Richard Wallace, Wally, as the boys called him, was tall for his age, with penetrating eyes and brown hair, parted to one side, which framed his foxy face in a perfect, boyish manner.

To my girlfriends' dismay, I was not attracted to him. At first, I pretended I couldn't understand English. He dismantled my pretense and I was quickly charmed. He offered me pieces of

English toffee, which his parents had given him as tuck food while at the boarding school. He kept the chocolate hidden in his uniform, in one of the side pockets of his gray trousers. We danced throughout the three hours of the dance, taking short breaks to drink sour lemonade or room temperature water, or to sit with our respective group of friends. Afterward, Richard wrote me love letters, which I read sprawled on my boarding school bed, closing my eyes to form a perfect picture in my head of whatever he described in the letter. We saw each other very little, *condicio sine qua non* for our growing mutual fascination, and for our imagined attachment to each other. Had we been able to see each other more frequently, the relationship promptly would have ground to standstill. The confinement of our respective boarding schools fed the urge and the excitement that surrounded every act that involved the other: the phone calls, the letters, the invitation to the school dances, the school holidays.

I still cannot put a finger on what made me stop fancying him. It happened suddenly and once it did there was no turning back. I started noticing all the grammar mistakes and punctuation errors in his weekly letters. The mere thought of English toffee made me sick to my stomach. The weekly letters began to lie unopened and unread. Towards the end, the very thought of his face became repugnant. I felt no guilt, no repentance of having severed all ties without an explanation. It was a done fact; I had broken his heart. Perhaps something my brother mentioned in one of his own letters, had been the deathblow. My brother said that Richard Wallace did not know how to defend himself when wrestling with the other boys, the words accompanied by a drawing of Richard dominated by another boy. Underneath the drawing he had written "SISSY" in red, capital letters.

It was not the first time I rejected a boy for appearing weak in front of others. At age four, I fell in puppy love with Luis Mariano, a five-year old boy in my prekindergarten class. I made my mother invite him and his three-year-old brother Neneo – to entertain my brother – to The Big House for a play date and cake. My fascination with Luis Mariano was cut short when, one day on the school playground, a bigger boy beat him in a fight. I couldn't get over the sight of him crying, defeated, standing by the slide. I stopped talking to him at once, refusing even to be seen next to him. In hindsight, it may have been the awakening of my desire for strength; the very opposite of what I saw in my own parents and their shortcomings.

***

At the time, I was unaware that 11-year-old girls are not supposed to be interested in boys, never mind capable of managing their advances and expectations, emotional or otherwise. Whether this precocity arose from the tortured interactions with my father or was the product of having suffered the permanent rupture of my family, I cannot say. I simply took the world as I found it, and in England the world was suddenly populated with boys, mostly older boys, who were interested in me. I declined to respond with fear, or shyness. The attention of boys, while puzzling, was also flattering, and fun, and I meant to meet it head on. Oh, how much I had to learn...

I met another boy on a camping trip to the Welsh countryside. His name was David Goodchild and his eyes were big, round, and a translucent blue. He was ever so charming and polite, and I decided I would fancy him. I was not yet driven by the romantic or sexual impulse, but merely went through the motions. David and I sat together by the campfire, sharing stories of arduous climbing on the Snowdonia mountain range, where I had once gotten lost and cried for hours, trying to find my way back to the camp, and of forbidden swims in the freezing mountainside streams. One night, we were sitting by the campfire when David Goodchild got up to use the bathroom. Quick as a dagger, my brother who had been sitting on the other side of the fire, ran to my side.

"Have you noticed how monstrously big David Goodchild's ears are?" he fervently whispered. The seed had been planted.

The next morning, I was sick to my stomach, having caught stream fever from drinking the water. Alone, lying in my tent, revolting thoughts of boys with big ears danced in my head. The charm had been irreparably broken.

How easily words poison the mind as the stream water had poisoned my body. My mother was a master at poisoning minds. She made sure any budding sprigs of self-esteem and pride in myself were nipped short before they even had a chance to grow. First, she delivered the initial blow that would open the wound: a casual negative comment, an unexpected malicious opinion. Then, she made sure the wound never healed by continuously pouring the stingy poison of hurtful comments into it.

My mother poisoned the way I viewed others. She poisoned the way I formed opinions. Most importantly, she poisoned my own image in my eyes. She did away with my self-esteem and in doing so, she suffocated my natural optimism and joy. It would take many years to undo the damage she inflicted upon my psyche.

What Doesn't Kill You Makes You Stronger

As different as my life had become in boarding school, my relationship with my mother remained a true constant. One frigid January afternoon, as the sun was beginning to set, my mother lost her composure with me during some silly quarrel at the English townhouse where she was staying. I cannot recall the subject of our conflict, but it pushed her into new realms of parental cruelty.

"You are the rudest, most disrespectful, and overall most disagreeable person I have ever known!" she shouted, "I want you out of my house!"

With that, she pushed me out the door and closed it securely behind me. I still wore my school uniform, having removed not so much as the school blazer. We were at odds from the moment I walked into her lodgings. It was the height of the English winter, and I was under dressed for the weather. Seeking refuge a few meters down the road in the community car garage, I hid in my mother's parking space, which was empty because she didn't own a car. I stayed there for almost four hours. My fingers stiffened with cold inside my navy blue school gloves. It started to snow outside.

Unable to stand the cold any longer, I walked back to the house and rang the doorbell. At once, my mother came to the door, holding the English version of the yellow pages in her hand.

"You are back," she said, not an ounce of regard in her oddly even tone.

"I only came back to watch my show on TV," I replied. "Top of the Pops, at 7:25."

She regarded me with crazed eyes for a moment before throwing the phone book at me. She missed. I tried to cross the doorsill, but she blocked me, again and again, and pushed me back out.

"You have to apologize before you can come in."

I apologized. I had to. It was either being humiliated at the hands of my mother or returning to the bitter cold outside. I chose the former, to preserve my life. This is not an exaggeration. I believe she would have allowed me to die of exposure had I not bowed to her demand for an apology.

As she moved aside to grant me entry, the phone rang. I ran inside to answer it. It was my grandmother, and her sweet warm, reassuring voice, just what I needed after the meaningless fracas with my mother. In the background, my mother murmured repeated threats that she would "make my life impossible" if I were to tell my grandmother she had kicked me out of the house in the middle of winter.

Tears coursed silently down my cheeks. I wanted to tell my grandmother everything, but I didn't dare. While she may have been a source of solace, she was thousands of miles away and my mother was right there with me. As I fought to contain the tears, my throat closed down on me, and I realized I had no one I could turn to. I was alone. I was utterly at the mercy of an out-of-control, deceptive, hyperemotional, unstable, and cruel woman who had no interest in her responsibilities as a mother. I was eleven years old and this was a devastating truth.

My grandmother, however, had welcome news. The trip she had been planning around my birthday was confirmed. She would fly to London to collect my brother and I sometime during the spring, partly coinciding with our half-term holiday. We would then spend three weeks in Israel and five days in Rome. Through her connections, she had secured us a private audience with Pope John Paul II. The idea of such a trip brought a smile to my wet face. I had something to look forward to and felt loved by one adult member of my family, at least.

To survive life with my mother, I had to split myself in two. A part of me lived permanently in the future, by devoting the totality of my time to intellectual and academic endeavors I would succeed in securing a less frightening life for myself. I believed this would be enough to save me. At the very least, it afforded me the illusion of some control over my life. I spent hours studying English grammar, reviewing French vocabulary, and practicing Latin declensions. The other part of me, the part that lived in the present, was frightened, alone, abandoned, and emotionally bereft.

That night, my mother went upstairs to her room and came down with a bottle of pills. I was sitting in the small dining room. She announced she was going to kill herself because of me. Sitting down, she emptied the bottle on the table. I looked at the small, white pills. She went to the kitchen for water.

"Do you know what I have here?" she demanded. "Do you know what these pills are for? These pills will take me out of this wretched life."

I looked back at her. She waited for me to say something, and then went on.

"Your father abandoned us. We have no money."

Then, one by one, she swallowed the pills.

"This is because of you," she said with each one. "This is all because of you."

I watched her in silence. Perhaps she had been waiting for me to spring up to knock the white pills from her hand, to hug her and tell her how much I loved her, and to please stop all the nonsense.

I didn't. Calmly, in the bizarre tranquility that desperation sometimes brings on, I stood up and opened the small book of addresses and telephone numbers that was by the phone, in the kitchen. I called Father Dominic O'Brien, the headmaster at my brother's school.

Father Dominic was an Irish priest and a renaissance man. My mother befriended him from the very beginning. She offered him invitations for dinner to the most expensive, exclusive restaurants in town, invitations that were never refused. The night of my mother's attempted suicide, he was the only adult I knew. Once I explained the situation, he was immediately on his way. He called the dispatching service for an ambulance to come to the house.

In the meantime, my mother had slumped to the floor, unconscious. I felt contempt and disdain for her thirty five year old body, lying motionless on the hard wooden floor, in silence. Not long after the phone call, the men from the ambulance were at the door. They rushed my mother to the hospital for a gastric lavage. Not wanting me to stay alone at the house, Father Dominic took me with him to my brother's boarding school in Godalming, in South East England, to spend the night. The room where I slept was clean and orderly, away from the boys' dormitories. I will never forget the look on my brother's face when the next morning, he saw me in the Refectory, at breakfast, sitting alone at a separate table. I satisfied his anxious curiosity with the truth. He looked at me with terror in his eyes, then he looked away, and finally, his gaze turned downwards, to the floor, where it remained for several minutes. It was as if he didn't know whose side to be on, whose pain to comfort: his sister's or our mother's. We hugged. And then he was gone for his lessons. My mother was discharged from the hospital that afternoon and I went back to her house. I could not consider it "home." To this day, she has not once ever spoken about what happened that night. Neither did my rescuer, Father Dominic. At this point my mother disgusted me. I did not want to be associated with her craziness and the lack of order in her life. Over the next several days, my emotional detachment from her was complete and final.

***

Father Dominic had not been alone in receiving my mother's invitations to posh restaurants. She took a liking to one of the neighbors. His rental townhome was directly opposite ours. Meneer Jarmo was of Dutch origin and spoke in heavily accented English. Rough in his mannerisms, he was short, balding, and sported an impressive moustache, a potbelly, and a deep love for gin, as the empty bottles all over his house attested. He quickly became a familiar figure in the house. For the second year of our stay in Europe, it was decided I would no longer be a boarder at the convent. I became a day student, returning home each afternoon. Coming in after school, I was disgusted to find him lying on our coach, snoring, and visibly inebriated.

A friend of a friend of Jarmo's had secured tickets to the races of Ascot, in Berkshire. He had of course invited my mother, who had been delighted to attend an event sponsored by the British Royal Family. She had been shopping for days to find the perfect hat for the occasion. Two days before the most prestigious race at the event, the King George VI and Queen Elizabeth Stakes which took place in July, I arrived from school to find Jarmo, once again, snoring on my mother's couch. I had invited a friend, Luisa, a half-Italian, half-Spanish girl my age, to stay with me for the weekend. Back in those days, I made a habit of inviting friends to the house to shield myself from my mother's anger and spite. She behaved better if someone else was there.

Luisa and I giggled as we listened to Jarmo's sodden concert. An hour later, he awakened from the slumber. He sat up on the coach and saw me in the kitchen with the telephone receiver in my hand, as I had been in the middle of dialing another friend's number.

He called out in a loud voice, "You have to ask your mother for permission to use the phone."

I could not believe my ears, the audacity of this man, this drunk from across the street. Informing Jarmo that he was not my father and had no rights over me, I continued making my phone call.

Jarmo raised his bulk from the couch and rushed toward me. I fled upstairs to hide in one of the bathrooms, the only room in the whole house that could be locked from the inside. He banged on the bathroom door.

"Come out!" he shouted. "Come out of there this instant!"

As told by my friend Luisa, he then went back downstairs, to the kitchen, where he opened a drawer and took out a sharp knife. He was going for the stairs again when Luisa cried out.

"I have never seen anything so cruel in my life!"

Jarmo stopped. He stood, frozen, at the bottom of the stairs, with the knife in his hand. He stared into nothingness as he opened his hand. The knife clattered to the floor. Turning, he looked at Luisa and stumbled from the house. It was quite a long time before I came out of my hiding place.

My mother had been home the entire time, in her room. I am not sure if she had been sleeping or hiding or simply nonchalant. I knew not to call out for her, not to ask her to help me or be on my side. Feeling alone, certain of my mother's refusal to ever protect me, I sobbed loudly, covering my face with my hands, embarrassed in front of Luisa, afraid. I will never forget what she said after Luisa told her what had just happened. She looked at me angrily.

"Now, because of you, because I have to 'protect' you," she said. "I can no longer see Jarmo, let alone go to the Ascot Races. It's all your fault!"

That night, Father Dominic called the house asking to talk to me. He told me he thought it was a very bad idea to tell my grandmother or anyone else about Jarmo and the knife. He said my mother would be very upset if she found out I had broken my silence, and that I would suffer the consequences. He never asked how I felt about the whole incident; let alone offered any counselling or even a prayer.

Once again, I felt utterly and helplessly alone. I came to realize that the only sensible adult in my life was no longer on my side. Luisa, who had practically saved my life, refused to set foot in my mother's house again.

"Luisa, come on," I begged at school, "I don't want to be alone with her!"

"I am sorry," she mumbled, looking away. I could not blame her for her unease but it was disappointing, nonetheless.

She blamed her mom for not giving her permission to come. We both knew it was a lie because Luisa had made very clear to me that she never told her mom anything about her life, let alone about her friends' lives. It was a white, comfortable lie that helped us navigate the survival of our friendship in the rough waters of my domestic life.

I began to stay at school long after it was time to go home. I would do all the homework that was due the following day and more. I read and reread all sorts of books; and went to the school chapel to pray before going home. I stayed out of my mother's way and she stayed out of mine. In the small two bedroom house, I avoided her completely. Contact was minimal; and other than a few polite exchanges in the evenings, (she would always be asleep in the mornings when I left for school) conversation was non-existent. I never watched Top of The Pops again.

***

I never told my grandmother about Jarmo, but not because of Father Dominic's warnings. It would have caused her a great deal of suffering. Sometime later, Father Dominic O'Brien left the priesthood. He had fallen in love with a Dutch woman, Ellen, the mother of one of the boys at school, and also my mother's friend. After she rejected him, he left to make a new life for himself in America. In an unselfish act of kindness, he took with him his protégé, a boy whose parents had dropped off at the boarding school and had never returned. Until the time of his departure and in spite of siding with my mother on occasion, Father Dominic remained a figure of stability and responsibility in my life.

My grandmother came in the springtime, as promised, together with two of my aunts and one of my cousins. The three weeks we spent travelling with her were both lifesaving and life giving. I treasure those weeks still, and constantly relive them. They were an oasis of beauty, comfort, security and spirituality in an otherwise bleak and anxious existence. I hugged my grandmother tightly, resting my head on her chest. I felt safe and protected as I closed my eyes and was able to let go and relax in the arms of a caring adult for the first time in many months.

The best gift a parent can give to a child is travel, taking them places, and those three weeks were a balm on the wounds of mistrust and betrayal, creating, even if only temporarily, a protective barrier to whatever further emotional insults I would be subjected to upon returning home to my mother. I cherished those twenty-one days, during which I did not have to worry about paying bills, booking hotels and tour guides, organizing day trips or planning meals and making reservations at restaurants. I just had to go along with the group, be present, take it all in, and savor each experience.

My grandmother booked us into five-star hotels and restaurants, which only enhanced the exposure to a wealth of different cultures and ideas. It also made me realize my mother's "crying poverty" was a most powerful weapon for exerting control through fear over her children. In Jerusalem, I reveled in hearing the Muslims called to prayer over loudspeakers, as Orthodox Jews incessantly and relentlessly, worshipped at the Wailing Wall. I spent hours pondering on the fact that a hotelier, in the center of Tel Aviv, would not serve me a chicken sandwich and a glass of milk together out of respect for Jewish law.

"But I am not Jewish!" I insisted, to no avail.

"It does not matter, Miss," he said. "You happen to be staying at a Jewish establishment and by the laws that govern it you must abide."

Swimming in the salty water of the Dead Sea brought a new meaning to the idea of floating, this time, effortlessly. The Masada Desert was mysterious, almost magical. My brother and I dreamt of devils and demons, tapping on our hotel window and knocking on our hotel room door. We reveled in the fascination and thrill of being frightened, in awe of our own night terrors and of St. Mark's and St. Luke's accounts of whatever exchange had taken place between Our Lord Jesus and Lucifer during the forty days and forty nights of fasting in the desert. We were immensely grateful we did not have to fast, as the food during the whole trip was delicious, particularly at the Kibbutz where we stayed. The lunch menu at the Kibbutz was fresh, wholesome and refreshingly simple.

To my delight, we sat with the people who lived there full-time, not merely with other tourists. The weather was perfect that day, a sunny, cool seventy degrees Fahrenheit, and I felt a thousand light years away from school. In the Garden of Gethsemane, we were mesmerized by the olive trees, imagining they were the very same trees under which Our Lord had wept the night He was betrayed. After all, according to the legend, "Olive trees never die."

***

As glorious as Israel may have been, Italy was the highlight of the trip. From the moment we landed at the Fiumicino airport, the air was laden with the scents of spring and heavy with the promise of rich, buttery Alfredo sauce. My grandmother had made a reservation at the supposedly original "Alfredo" restaurant in Rome. Even if it had been a tourist trap, my brother and I did not care, devouring the perfectly al dente linguini drenched in the heavenly sauce. Every morning we took our breakfast in our room, at the Luxurious Grand Hotel Plaza, close to the Spanish Steps. My brother and I loved to sit outside, on the room terrace overlooking the busy streets, the sound of Vespa engines humming in the air, serving as the perfect background to our stay in the Eternal City.

On the morning of April the twentieth, 1982, my grandmother drew a special bath for me. I had turned twelve years old. My special bath marked the beginning of a memorable day, not only for me, being my birthday, but for everyone else in the group. It was the morning of our semi-private audience with the Pope. My grandmother and several of her sisters, my great aunts, the same women who had woven incredible tales of my father's drug dependency and the black magic spells that his lover had supposedly cast on him, had secured connections with the Roman Curia through numerous ecclesiastical ties back in South America. Bishops, Cardinals, priests and seminarists were among the hoard of Very Important Persons that frequently came over to The Big House for exquisite meals. All those evenings, heavy with wine and cheer, had finally paid off, delivering the perfect reward for the faithful worshippers: an audience with the Holy Father. An audience that would be brimming with the indulgences brought on not only by the Sanctifying Papal Visit in itself, but by the fact that 1982 had been designated a Jubilee Year. To gain the additional indulgences brought on by the Jubilee, we just had to make sure to go through the appropriately designated doors and entryways in the Holy City of the Vatican.

I dressed humbly for the occasion, dizzy from the anticipation of being made Holy and of all my sins being forgiven, a veritable passport to Heaven. What more could a twelve-year-old Catholic girl want for her birthday? We waited in a private room, in silence, for the Pope to appear. The group included a family of South American tourists, a delegation of Italian master gold-smiths and their wives, and us.

And then, the Pope finally arrived. One by one, for a few minutes, he spoke to each of us. The couple in line before me, one of the goldsmiths and his wife told the Pope that the black crucifix they were holding in their hands talked. I shall never forget the smile on His Holiness's face, as he dismissed the woman, with his reply: "Que parla, parla italiano?" ("What does it speak, does it speak Italian?"). The couple laughed nervously as they walked away. When our turn came, my brother and I flew at him. He opened his arms wide to welcome us with a hug and a blessing. It was the best feeling in the world: We were Holy. We had been made Holy, and as strange as it may seem, the presence of the Pope, his devotion to the Virgin Mary, awakened in me a desire to feel connected to whatever gave the Holy Father such peace and tranquility. The connection, alas, wore off after only a few nights. I soon stopped praying. Many years passed before I would find anything like what I felt in the papal presence.

Why did I stop praying? Youth? The desire for the immedi-ate answering of my prayers, which the wisdom of maturity has taught me happens in God's own time?

I was praying for outcomes: for my parents to get back together, for my mother to act less crazily. The intention in my prayers was to change the external, not the internal. Needless to say, I did not see any changes in my outer circumstances. Frustrated and in despair, I allowed the habit of prayer to fall away. I lacked the insight to aspire to a personal connection with Divinity, with Source. I was too young to understand that what determines our sense of well-being and happiness is not so much how the external circumstances in our lives affect us. It lies much more in the way our inner circumstances determine the way in which we respond to our outer lives. The internal world is of paramount importance, compared to the material world around us.

I failed to learn this lesson from my interaction with the Pope. At twelve, I fell out of touch with my spiritual nature albeit temporarily.

***

As the trip drew to a close, I did not want to return to the United Kingdom. I wanted to stay in Rome, learn Italian, and work in the kitchen of any of those restaurants. I also wanted to stay in Israel, become a vegetable grower and live in a Kibbutz, organically and peacefully. I could perhaps speak to a Rabbi and be allowed to do my part at the Wailing Wall. I had stared and stared at the writing in Hebrew, on the signs in the streets and in the menus of restaurants, at the pages that read from right to left, and the books that opened from back to front.

It was a peace of 21 days and this holiday with my grandmother had decongested my stuffed-up soul, it had healed me through and through, and I never wanted it to end.

Damage

I will never forget the day we took the train to London. I had just turned thirteen. My brother and I had taken up tennis at our respective schools, and my Mother wanted to buy us tennis racquets and balls. She thought Hamley's, the toy department store in London, would be an excellent purveyor of sporting goods. I was anxious over the consequences of our "new poverty", kept evergreen by my mother's ceaseless denouncements of my absent father, and I am sure my brother was too. We secretly wondered and asked each other how long we thought our grandmother's money would last. She spotted the tennis racquets once we reached the top floor of the department store. She gathered up five of them, as if collecting firewood, or picking flowers. I was alarmed at the sight, and the thought of the expense, given that my brother and I were only two players. If we happened to befriend other players at school, we would have been four players, at most.

"Why are you buying so many racquets when you only have two children?" I asked.

The answer came quickly, in the form of furious, alternating slapping: right, left, right.

"I will do whatever I want!" she screamed at the top of her lungs.

Soon a pair of store security guards joined us. "Is everything okay?"

I was sobbing uncontrollably. Not only did my face hurt from the strength of her entire arm concentrated on the palm of her slapping hand, but also from the red markings that the big, heavy rings she wore left on my face.

"Everything is perfectly all right," my mother said with a big smile. The security guards looked at us, but my mother was allowed to pay for the tennis gear and depart the story without further questions.

This was a demonstration of my mother's uncanny capacity for alternating her mood at will. It was her own special kind of superpower. She beguiled many a police officer out of giving her a speeding ticket by switching on one of her personas. She would start to cry as soon as the police officer approached our car. She would then concoct a horrifying tale of how she had been driving over the speed limit because her son was at the hospital, dying from acute leukemia. The speed at which the lies flew from her mouth was mystifying.

That night, we arrived home with five tennis racquets in our shopping bags. It was the week before Christmas. We made the mistake of asking my mother if we were going to see our father for the holidays or if at least he had sent us any Christmas gifts. Instantly she flew into a furious rage, crying loudly and uncontrollably, like a small child. She assaulted my brother, who sat on the floor by the small, artificial Christmas tree, kicking him in the legs and the groin with her expensive stiletto boots. My brother tried to scramble away, still sitting on the floor, dragging himself backwards with his arms.

He let out a cry, "Where is God? Where is God?"

Indeed, where was God when we had most needed Him? I had often wondered the same thing myself.

That night we cried ourselves to sleep, yet again.

Come morning, we stayed in our rooms for as long as possible, terrified to come out and face her. At around noon, unexpectedly, a soft knocking came on the door. It was my mother, her hands full of gifts, of boxes that she had stayed up all night wrapping. She was on her knees, crying, apologizing, begging for forgiveness. My brother and I had looked at each other, not knowing what to expect. To this day, I am convinced the apology came through only because it was my brother who had been assaulted and at that time it made me miss my sister. It made me long for our togetherness; the shared misery of being born of the wrong sex in my mother's eyes.

***

During our time in England, we accompanied my mother on several trips to spots throughout Europe. Summer holidays we spent in the south of Spain, in Andalucía, a time always filled with unpredictability and scandal. My mother slept till one or two in the afternoon. My brother and I walked around, by ourselves, admiring the beauty and luxury of the Melia Don Pepe in Marbella. The daughter of Julio Iglesias, Chabeli, who was my same age, together with one of her brothers, was staying there, along with other celebrities that I recognized from years of reading the Spanish gossip magazines, "Hola" and "Semana." I obtained an autograph from a very famous bullfighter, Francisco Paquirri, who would tragically die from wounds inflicted by a bull some eighteen months later. The lift stopped inadvertently on a higher floor, and in walked the bullfighter, dressed in the most beautiful "suit of lights" I had ever seen. We travelled down together for several floors, before emerging onto the mezzanine together. I beseeched him to wait a moment while I secured a pen and a piece of paper, any piece of paper (I found a cocktail napkin) for an autograph and could not believe my luck.

One morning in Marbella, my mother wanted to go to the bank. We took a taxi to one of the local branches of the English bank where she kept her money. She identified herself and first asked for a balance of the account. To her dismay, the clerk announced an exorbitant amount of money. We were all confused. My mother had never had such an amount of funds in the bank. The clerk requested identification for the second time. She was, indeed, Senora Michelena (as she had decided to keep my father's surname for our sake), but the name on the account belonged to a different Senora Michelena. The other authorized name on the account was my father's. Yes, my father had opened a faraway, offshore account for the new woman in his life and had deposited an astronomical sum in it.

My mother erupted in hysterics. She slid on her sunglasses to shield herself from the embarrassment and proceeded to damn my father to the "Special Affairs" clerk and anyone else who seemed to be interested. She went into bouts of shrieks, her body trembling. Discovering the new account was the maximal betrayal by her ex-husband, my father. She did not want to admit it, but she was still very much in love with him. Sometimes she would wear a special perfume, a sweet yet elegant fragrance that my father had given her and, in oblivion, would announce to us and to the world: "My husband gave me this perfume when I finally bore him a son! Isn't it the most delicious thing you have ever smelled? My husband has impeccable taste."

Embarrassed and made self-conscious by this public display, I asked her to pull herself together, to act like an adult. Instantly I became the focus of her rage. She slapped me, declaring I was evil and no fit companion. Unfair? Yes—but at least, now she was angry, which was better than hysterical and helpless.

Or so I thought.

After visits to the Alhambra and Generalife, architectural treasures surviving from the 800 years of Islamic domination of the Iberian Peninsula, I became transfixed by Moorish culture. At all times I carried with me a copy of Washington Irving's *Tales of the Alhambra,* essays and sketches from the author's 1828 visit to Granada. A romantic account that combined historical events and myth, it was the perfect companion. Knowing what an avid reader her granddaughter was, my grandmother had recommended it to me. My reading of the book was perfectly timed to the vacation, and it lasted me precisely the exact duration of the trip. I read the last page of the book as we waited to board the plane back to the United Kingdom.

Sometimes my mother went on trips by herself, with friends, leaving me alone at the house to fend for myself. When I was thirteen, during one of her absences, while she met a friend from South America at some Parisian festival, I became very ill. I developed an acute case of colitis. The pain was so severe that simply lying still on my bed became an ordeal. I twisted and writhed like a pretzel from the pain. I called the hotel in Paris where she was staying. Once again, she summoned Father Dominic, who took me to the hospital, where they gave me pills and tests. The pain in my abdomen was successfully lessened but not the pain in my heart. I wanted my mother by my side, whatever that meant. Despite her emotional instability and random cruelty, I missed whatever miserly crumbs I was accustomed to receiving. I missed her, not with the innocent naivete of a younger child but rather one on the verge of adolescence who could understand that perhaps I missed who she might have been too.

I made a full recovery in time to begin planning and preparing for our trip home, our return to our native country of Venezuela.

I calculated the balance in my head. The thirty months spent abroad had been brutal. In one column, I listed my academic achievements, and my total immersion in the Anglo Saxon culture, which I valued highly. In the other column, the time spent alone, dealing with my mother with no other adult in sight, which had wrenched an emotional toll on me. I did not savor the thought of returning to the private Catholic school where I knew a million personal questions lay dormant, ready to wake up and annihilate any self-confidence or sense of adequacy I had acquired while abroad. I recited Yeats in my mind, "I balance all, brought all to mind, the years to come seem waste of breath, a waste of breath the years behind, in balance with this life, this death." I was my own bookish companion, the only companion I had then.

My apprehension about life back at the Ursuline Academy was not misplaced. I now spoke in the manner of an English boarding school girl, the Queen's English, so to say. The other girls spoke American English. A lot of them travelled frequently to their vacation homes or flats in the Southeast portion of the United States. Many spent their summer at camp in New England, sent there to improve their command of the English language. At once I became the object of cruel jokes and mockery because of my accent. I was tormented for my hairstyle, now in an English "mod" cut, and for the bright pink or blue tights and boots I wore outside of school. Deep down, I was very happy to have been accepted back at the Ursuline Academy. It was an academically topnotch school and that gave me a sense of security. But my day-to-day life was difficult. I became introverted, timid, and quite shy around everybody

A shock awaited us when we returned from Europe. The Big House was no longer ours. My uncle and my grandmother had sold it over the summer, in an effort to reduce the family's cost of living. It was to be a part of a complex of buildings that would become an assisted living facility for the elderly. We never even got a chance to say goodbye to The Big House. My grandmother moved to an apartment, ten minutes away. The apartment had belonged to her mother. It was there that we were all supposed to live together, happily ever after: my grandmother, my mother, my sister, my brother, the maid and myself. The apartment had three bedrooms, plus a room for the maid, by the kitchen. However, my brother and I did the math in our heads, whichever combination of people and beds in rooms we played with, the indisputable conclusion had been that there would never be any privacy or space for either one of us. My sister had gotten a room, all to herself, so had my mother. My brother and I had to share the remaining room with my grandmother—or, God Bless her, she had been forced to share her room with her two adolescent grandchildren.

My grandmother drove us to school every morning. She arose very early, at five in the morning, to shower and powder herself. She was impeccable in her style, always carrying herself in a distinguished manner. She also dosed herself in heavy French perfume, Shalimar, Chanel No. Five and others. My brother and I woke up sneezing madly. We did not have to get up for another hour yet we lay awake, in the darkness, sneezing. As for my sister, she was happily attending college, as in a couple of hours in the morning, and then off to the beach with her friends she went. My sister was the kind of person who needed guidance and motivation, preferably from someone who could be firm, yet soft-spoken and nurturing. What my sister needed was a mother, or at the very least, a motherly figure.

What she got was my grandmother, who took a harsh tone towards her. My relationship with my grandmother was far easier and we got along superbly. We had many things in common, a love for books and travel, very strong personalities and a passion for the beach club. We were both extremely industrious and inventive.

When it had been time for me to come out into society, customarily celebrated with a grand quinceañera party thrown by parents when girls reached the age of fifteen, my grandmother offered to organize one for me. She gave me the option of my own debutante ball or a chaperoned trip to Europe with other girls from local, private high schools. I chose the latter, in spite of having already travelled plenty around Europe. Even though I never had my own party, my grandmother personally dropped me off and picked me up at the other girls' parties to which I had been invited.

As for the dresses I wore to these events, she personally saw to it that I selected a suitable, age-appropriate model, usually out of a fashion magazine, after which we went shopping together at a store specializing in luxury fabrics and materials for dressmaking. My grandmother insisted on colorful, shiny taffeta or beautiful velour for my dresses. The last step, which was also the step that I enjoyed the most, entailed taking the fabric and the fashion magazine that would serve as inspiration to Giovanna, my grandmother's dressmaker. Giovanna was an Italian seamstress my grandmother had found by word of mouth. These dressmaking excursions with my grandmother constituted the only occasions, from girlhood to adult independence, when someone designed and created something special, just for me. In an adult world of ready-to-wear, I still miss the process of researching an idea for a dress, picking out high-quality fabric, and delivering it all to a dressmaker who would create a beautiful indulgence.

My grandmother's presence, despite her attitude toward my sister, softened the reality of our new life at the apartment. The Spanish gossip magazines that had been religiously delivered to The Big House every Friday afternoon, came no more. The delivery of local newspapers also came to an end. I loved to read, and those periodicals from my childhood provided solace and entertainment, and would have undoubtedly been helpful in my quest to escape life at the overcrowded apartment, if not physically, at least psychologically.

My mother fought constantly with my grandmother, over all manner of things: big things, little things. The volume and the heavy emotional charge of their arguments quickly escalated past uncomfortable to the unbearable. They paid no heed to my brother and me, as we sat there, staking in every word. Neither cared if we were trying to study, to do homework, or perhaps just trying to listen to music, or have a conversation with each other:

What came out of my grandmother's mouth and my mother's mouth in return was a barrage of profanity and personal insult. It was almost impossible to believe that two well-bred, elegant adults could fall prey to the most despicable of impulses and behaviors, and stoop so low in front of the children.

One afternoon my mother received the big news that she would have to find a job and work for a living. She was in shock. She was truly devastated by the thought of having to set an alarm clock, get up at a decent hour, drive to work, and do something in her life that did not involve a manicure or pedicure, the hair salon or shopping. She had openly and blatantly refused to find an occupation. The bearer of these unwelcome tidings was my uncle. After my grandfather's death, he was determined to protect my grandfather's patrimony. Having worked all his life, beginning in high school, he had been of the opinion that it would be highly beneficial mentally and physical for my mother to do something with her life—find a job, get out of the apartment, to get a life.

My uncle rang her up one afternoon to broach the subject. He was not willing to fund my mothers' luxuriant life from the inheritance they shared. Her response was swift and brutal.

In a fit of rage and unfounded resentment, she yelled at my uncle.

"I know you! I know what this is all about!"

"I want only what is best for everyone," he said.

"You want me to walk the streets and earn my living as a prostitute, as a *whore!*"

She said all this in front of us, over the phone, in a conversation with her brother, my uncle, that should have been held in private, if at all. Her half of the conversation was more than enough to incite anxiety in us. No one seemed to care we were there, looking on, listening. As soon as my mother slammed down the receiver, hanging up on my uncle, my grandmother started quizzing her about the phone conversation, twisting it accordingly to make room for her own distorted assessment of the situation.

"My daughter is a whore," she shouted, completely misunderstanding. "She is a prostitute on the streets! My daughter is a whore!"

What followed was a forceful, physical encounter between mother and daughter. They grabbed each other by the hair while ugly, crude and hurtful phrases shot out from their lips. My mother resorted quickly to her favorite threat.

"I am going to kill myself," she screamed, pulling away from my grandmother and leaning toward the windows. 'I am going to throw myself off the balcony!"

Given her previous suicide attempt, I was alarmed. I knew there was a gun in the apartment, in my grandmother's closet safe, and I knew my mother locked herself up in my grandmother's room for hours at a time. Guns were nothing foreign to her, having already used one on my father at the Beach Club, where she had fortunately missed. Or unfortunately, depending on who you asked.

By dinner, my mother and grandmother were teasing and gossiping with each other like always but my anxiety did not diminish. I knew she was capable of anything, of inflicting real injury to others and to herself. The overcrowding and the constant fighting at the apartment were taking a toll on all of us. We were like rats in a too-small cave. Something had to give.

Mercifully, for all involved, a suitable job fell on my mother's lap. Before his death, when my mother was a young woman, my grandfather insisted that she secure a degree from a well-respected university. She chose the Universidad Metropolitana, where she earned a degree in foreign languages, and her syllabus had included the study of literature and poetry. As a result, she possessed the credentials for teaching. Those credentials made her a very attractive candidate for the job opportunity that had suddenly become available. It involved teaching Spanish and French to a certain Mr. El Hibri, a well-to-do gentleman of Arab origin, well versed in both diplomacy and business.

It would be at this job, that my mother was introduced to her future second husband. Another teacher at the same agency, a younger woman, thought my mother a wonderful match for her recently divorced father. Although exiled since the early nineteen sixties in the United States, he had remained true to his Latin roots. He had started to study law in Cuba, before the Revolution. Once in the safety of North America, he never pursued a formal degree. He ventured instead into the hospitality business, eventually owning a Cuban restaurant that had been moderately successful for a while. He also owned a boat. When he met my mother though, he had been in the middle of declaring bankruptcy and planning a move to the state of Virginia, to live for a while with his older brother, a successful pediatrician, and his family. Osito, as we would affectionately call him, was a kind, generous, spiritual, life-loving man. He was patient. He was forgiving.

Compounding the tragedy of his divorce, given that he was a true family man and also very religious, was the fact that his wife of twenty years had left him for another woman. He had mistakenly picked up the phone at his house to make a call and listened to a conversation between his wife and her lover, a well-known, high-society, Cuban lesbian. My mother agreed to fly to Florida to meet him. It was love at first sight. His romanticism and old-world manners charmed her at once, while her class, intelligence and sensibility, framed by her beauty and elegance, disarmed him.

Their courtship, though complicated by distance, was short. She visited him constantly, flying from Venezuela to the United States, during the short period that elapsed before their marriage two months later. There had been long conversations on the phone. She hid under her bed, so that her mother, my grandmother wouldn't be able to listen in or comment on the conversation. It made for a pitiful picture: an adult woman, no longer young, with three children, hiding under the bed to talk to her boy-friend. The courtship was attended by more fighting between her and my grandmother.

It became an even more unsustainable and unhealthy situation. My mother snapped at us for no reason. She started intervening in my life, randomly interfering with social activities. Once she called me into her bedroom and announced that I was grounded for the day.

"For what reason?" I demanded.

"Because I am your mother and I feel like it, and you have no choice but to accept my word and comply with my wishes."

By this time, I was on the cusp of adolescence, and though I feared her fierce, unexpected slaps, sometimes I could not contain myself.

"You're just miserable and bitter because you can't be with your boyfriend all the time!"

She gave me a look of malice, but there was new interest in it, too.

"What do you know of it? You are a child."

"You have to ruin everything," I said. "Always. My own mother can never be happy for me."

"You? What do you have to be happy about?"

"I'm doing well at school. The other girls like me. Well, most of them. Boys notice me whether I want them to or not. I'm happy everywhere but here at home! You insist everyone be as bitter and miserable as you."

My hand flew to cover my mouth. I had crossed a line, and I knew it. My shoulders hunched imperceptibly, my body prepared for the slapping that was sure to follow. But it did not come. Instead, my mother cast a cold eye upon me.

"You are grounded for a week."

I bit back my response. Going deeper into this territory would only bring more severe punishment on my head. I met my mother's gaze, looking her full in the face, not even blinking, for what seemed five minutes, six. Then I turned and silently left her room.

***

Not that I was the only one who suffered. We were over-crowded, yet isolated. We never sat at the table together for meals. We never shared any stories, like a normal family does. In reaction to the reigning neuroticism, we all kept to ourselves. Everybody was afraid of everybody else. There was no "How was your day?", no joking, no laughter, no lightness, ever. On any given day, we never knew what might set my mother off, or even more frightening, what would set off an argument between her and my grandmother. The mood was serious, somber, heavy with criticism, judgment, and mockery. "You are going out without a purse?" my grandmother asked my sister. "Are you a common, lowly woman on her way to her market stall?" Or, "How many men do you think you are going to get today with that short skirt you were wearing?" If she happened to see my sister drinking water in the kitchen, she was quick to say: "You drink too much water! You drink water like a damned toad!"

My sister often left the apartment in tears. She started to do poorly in college, as increasingly she skipped class altogether to go to the beach with her friends. I worried. Every time I saw her and my grandmother in the same room I was overcome by apprehension. I could sense my sister's anxiety and fear too. I don't recall ever hearing any word of praise from any of the adults at home towards her. There was never a kind gesture, never an encouraging word for her. In addition, she and I were not close. She could not relate to my bookishness and I could not relate to her college partying ways.

One topic in particular became the favorite target of both my grandmother and mother. This was my sister's boyfriend. He was seven years older than she was, an engineer by trade. Soft spoken, well mannered, and kind, he was precisely what my sister needed. He adored her. What would have been perfect in any parents' eyes for their child was not good enough for my mother or grandmother. They invited him to go out to dinner with them, only to later criticize his choices in food. "Your boyfriend is so common! The only thing he knows to order is Caesar Salad! Doesn't he know how to eat anything else?" They criticized his style of clothing, his shirts, his jeans. All his clothes were passé, to hear my mother and grandmother tell it. He was almost the only matter on which they agreed.

Soon enough my mother and grandmother succeeded in driving the poor man out of my sister's life. They drove my sister out of the apartment and out of our lives, too. Once she and the boyfriend were no longer associated, my sister became a stranger at home. She no longer talked to us, any of us. She would leave early in the morning and return late at night, until the night she failed to come home at all. My sister was gone for two months and we were all worried. We had no idea where she was.

We did not learn for a long time that she had taken off to the mountains, to become a pilgrim of a folkloric goddess, Maria Lionza, principal deity of a Venezuelan indigenous religion. She travelled with a group of bohemian friends, following in the footsteps of the Maria Lionza worshippers, who fell somewhere between santeros and shamans.

My sister followed them up the mountain range in the state of Yaracuy, all the way into Sorte, to the Altar Mayor or Principal

Altar, joining in the traditional dances over coals and the sacri-
ficing of animals. My sister came to revere lesser deities, as well:
La Negra Matea, the slave who was Simon Bolivar's nanny and
wet nurse, and Negro Primero, the first black man who had joined
the military ranks to fight the Spanish in our Independence War.

As a result of my sister's disappearance, my father tried to
contact us for the first time since our return from abroad. There
were no excited hellos or goodbyes during our short phone
conversation. He merely said he had contacted the police and
two private detectives, to help find my sister. Colleagues at work
kept asking him where his daughter was, as news had spread,
and he was embarrassed by the whole affair. I listened to him
carefully and attentively, hoping to detect an inflection in his
voice, a hesitation, a suggestion of fearing for my sister's life...
unfortunately, his delivery was flat and emotionless. In the end,
neither the police nor the two private investigators were able to
find her. She disappeared into thin air, and she would reappear
out of the blue. Unfortunately, she was no prodigal son, or in this
case, no prodigal daughter, in the eyes of my mother or grandmother. Even I had difficulty feeling any joy or happiness upon
her return, no empathy for what had driven her away, despite
witnessing her daily torture at the hands of my grandmother,
and my mother. The only feeling I was able to muster had been
one of profound relief; as I had truly feared for her life; mixed
with a heightened sense of anxiety about the oncoming high
drama now that she was back at the small apartment.

During this time, apart from the disappearance of my sister,
my mother was choking on her own desperation and despair.
She appeared emotionally trapped, secluded, and confined to a
small room and a telephone; all the men in her life were now
gone. Her doting father had been dead for some years now. Her
ex-husband, my father, wanted nothing to do with her. My
brother was in high school, even though on account of his age,

he shouldn't have been, and had signed up for after school activities that would include Saturday mornings. He spent much of his time at other people's houses—and who could blame him?

Still, we were children, and we never lost hope of a reconciliation between my father and my mother. I even once organized a rendezvous, calling my father to ask him to meet my mother at a local restaurant. He agreed, to my surprise. On the day of the "date," I was too excited to concentrate on my homework. In Europe, every one of the three wishes my brother and I made whenever we crossed the entryway of a new church (wishes that were guaranteed to be granted), was for our parents to be reunited. None of the wishes had come true, but I clung to hope. Hope is the last thing one gets to lose, especially children.

The meeting did not go well. He assented to the meeting only because he was quarreling with his mistress. My father was still involved with his lover, the one he had left his family for. According to my mother, not once did he stop talking about the other woman during dinner. My mother's disappointment was fathomless. She was irreparably heartbroken. There was no daddy to give her spending money anymore, no expensive new shoes or jewelry to be had. No husband to parade at the social soirees. At that point, the only consolation life provided her came in the form of the challenges inherent in a long-distance relationship. She clung to it in desperation. She wrote long love letters and sat in her room all day by the phone, like a condemned prisoner, waiting for the call that would set her free. Sometimes it came, and then she would be lighthearted for the duration of the conversation.

To help her cope, she resorted to a tranquilizing remedy, some natural herb recommended to her by a friend or a healer, but it had a disturbing secondary effect. All day long my mother went without putting a morsel of food in her mouth. Then, come four or five in the afternoon, she would drive to the local

"European Style" pastry shop, bringing home at least two, sometimes three, trays of French pastries. She gorged on the sweets, washing it all down with the blackest, bitterest of coffees. To my mind these treats, made of flour, lard and sugar, constituted a kind of prisoner's last meal. The pastries had almost no nutritional value, no matter how many she consumed. She grew to be malnourished, to look cachectic, a gigantic head atop an insanely thin body.

Apart from her romantic malaise, she had lost all of her friends, as the male-dominated traditional Venezuelan society idolized divorced men, while scapegoating discarded wives. Her friends now wanted nothing to do with her, not least because they feared she might spread her fate like a contagious disease. She was summarily dismissed from her usual circles. I don't know if it was God or the universe or life itself that was testing her, trying her strength, her ability to survive. All I know is that she failed, miserably.

There Will Be Scars

On the day the final insult arrived, like an unwelcome guest, we had lived in the apartment for several months. My mother, who had not gone to bed the night before, picked a fight over my sister's failed nose jobs which had taken place four years earlier, while my father was still at home, before the divorce. It is true that my sister's two plastic surgeries pleased no one. The first operation was botched by a not-very-competent surgeon who removed too much cartilage from her nasal bridge leaving her with a bobbed nose, like a Pekinese puppy. A second procedure to transplant cartilage from her ears to her nose finally gave her some semblance of a normal nose. It was partially successful.

The argument got out of hand quickly. My mother attempted to kick my sister out of the apartment. Instead of leaving, my sister locked herself in her room. My mother snapped. In her nightgown, she rampaged through the apartment, trashing the entire place. With exaggerated movements and gestures, she threw every piece of decoration, every plate, every ornament, furiously onto the floor. She found a heavy kitchen axe that the maid used to cut through pieces of bone and applied it to the door of my sister's room. My brother, the only voice she might listen to, begged her to stop. She abandoned the kitchen axe and my sister's door but proceeded to overturn the heavy table that my grandmother kept at the entrance of the apartment. The table fell to the floor with a deafening crash, cracking the marble floor. I watched this display in silence, in the same way I had watched her try to kill herself when I was eleven.

My grandmother called one of our cousins, a seminarist at the time, begging him to come to the apartment to talk some sense into her. Arturo, the priest-to-be, arrived within fifteen minutes.

He desperately tried to help. All my mother did was mock him and laugh at him, telling him that he was an idiot, and that he would fail in life as a priest because he didn't know how to speak! (On the contrary, my cousin went on to attain the rank of Principal of The Jesuit Order for the region of South America.) That day, she defeated every effort made by each and all of us to calm her down. She was unrestrained with a rage that wanted to burn ever hotter, with no interest in being quenched. She was a danger to herself and to everyone around her.

At last my uncle called an ambulance from a psychiatric hospital. The paramedics had to dart her, like some wild animal. Only then could she be brought under control. They took her away. We were left with the ruin of her anger, her destruction, and the sudden quiet of her absence.

Dismissing the whole incident as one more episode by my crazy mother, I continued to be the straight A student at school, burying all signs of the emotional terrorist at home. I wanted no one to know of the chamber of horrors that was my home. In that regard the strategy worked, but it left me alone with the traumatic aftermath. I had no levelheaded adult to talk with, to seek some form of guidance from, no one to provide perhaps a less anguished, more positive outlook than I could muster on my own. I knew nothing but the world formed in the orbit of my mother's illness, and in the damaged family that engendered her. I had no access to an alternate vision of what life could and should be like.

What little self-esteem and self-love I had managed to accrue vanished amid the ruins of the apartment once my mother was taken away. More than ever I tried to fill up the hole in my spirit by keeping to myself and working hard. I carried all this with me, the damage and the coping strategy, into adulthood. All so I did not have to feel too much or think too much about what lay beneath the surface, about my mother, or my father, or the circumstances of my childhood.

A few days after my mother entered the hospital against her will, her fiancé arrived. He made the astonishing decision, which seemed to me the most Christian of charities, to take my mother home with him to the United States. At the apartment, he explained. "I am not taking your mother away; I am just borrowing her for a little while." He promised us he would always stay with her; he would never abandon her as my father had done. A tinge of happiness and excitement flared inside me. If my mother was not coming back, then I would inherit her room. The overcrowding and lack of privacy would lessen. At that moment I felt an immense gratitude toward this man. For my mother, I felt nothing. I was not sad she was leaving, having finally reached my breaking point.

At school, the other girls developed a keen interest in my mother's whereabouts and personal life. From the safe platform of their parent's stable marriages they cast their darts at me. "Where is your mother?" one asked. I said she was away, in the United States, working. Another insisted, "Are you sure? My mother told me otherwise. My mother says your mother has a lover." I felt the tale-tell flush on my cheeks reminding me I was lying. "I am sure. Why would I lie to you?" I felt I was being crucified, up on a scaffold, for every girl, every teacher, and every nun to see. Only the passage of time eased their morbid fascination with my mother. Their hurtful questioning died away and the school became my sanctuary. I was thriving academically and I finally felt at ease socially. This ability to derive some satisfaction from doing well at school kept me going despite the gruesome realities of my family life. To the rest of the family, my mother's departure was the elephant in the room, a necessary evil, an inevitable outcome. Once gone, she never came up in any conversation. No one missed her. Not even her own mother.

I avoided talking to my mother after she left. I could not bring myself to listen to her little girl voice over the phone. I had grown tired of being the adult in the relationship. In the two years that followed, I had spoken to my mother on the phone just once, at my uncle's request.

In a stroke of impulsivity, after a brief courtship, (not quite two months, I believe) my mother remarried. She called, excited like a teenager, wanting to share her happiness with us. I wanted nothing to do with her. I could not physically bring myself to speak with her. My uncle, that fair and honorable man, sat me down on his lap, hugged me, and asked me to congratulate my mother on her marriage, explaining how important it was for my mother to know that I was happy for her. I sat on his lap, choking on my own tears, uttering the word "congratulations" and handing the receiver back to my uncle, unable to stomach her reply. My sister and my brother congratulated her with ease. I could not. Why should I want to mend the rift that she had caused? Something was broken inside of me, and I knew it was she who had broken it.

***

My grandmother's vascular dementia took a sharp turn for the worse. The natural cruelty she had always reserved for my mother and my sister in her younger years became the dominant trait of her personality. Her hypertension and diabetes were taking their toll. Her senility fed on the walls of the vessels that had been damaged by her uncontrolled blood pressure and diabetes. The dementia made it more difficult to control her sugar habit, nor did it help her with remembering to take her blood pressure pills. She would get up in the middle of the night and climb up on a stool to steal sugar from the top shelf of the cabinet where my brother and I had hidden the sugar canister. She would steal bottles of beer from the refrigerator, open them and pour eight, ten spoonsful of sugar in them. Slowly but surely, she was losing her mind. Of all the adults who had felt burdened by us children and had left us behind, she was the last one to leave but it hadn't been willingly. She left while she was still here. Her sanity went away, and only a shell remained.

I continued sharing a room with my grandmother. My brother got my mother's room instead of me. Her worsening dementia eroded filters of empathy and compassion, particularly with her loved ones. I was now sixteen, with my first official boyfriend, Konstantin. He was two years older than me, and in addition to being an excellent student, he was a professional athlete, competing for the country in pole vaulting. He was very, very tall, six feet and four inches to my five feet and two inches, and very handsome. Money for our movie outings and dinner dates came from the commercial television advertisements he participated in.

He was still in high school when we started dating but had already been accepted at a very prestigious science/math oriented university, Universidad Simon Bolivar. He came from a solid family and they took me on family vacation trips to California, where his mother was from, and around the Venezuelan countryside. Looking back on those anxiety filled years, it stands out that Konstantin fulfilled a companionship need. What has always remained unclear for me is the depth and the level of connection that a couple of adolescents can attain and maintain long term, and whether said connection will be able to survive and thrive into adulthood and into the golden years. Konstantin and I never had a deep connection…we just kept each other company for a few years. It is my belief that although we shared an academic and athletic ambition, we were still trying to find out who we (ourselves) were at the time. There is so much to learn and understand about oneself, and at sixteen, the door to introspection and self-knowledge is barely starting to open. I firmly believe that in our heart of hearts we both knew we would not be together in the end and today, it breaks my heart to see heart-school sweethearts holding on to the dream of ending up

together; particularly while surviving a long distance relationship as they head to opposite areas of the country in their pursuit
of a college education. My heart breaks specially for the girl, as
women have the capacity to hold onto people and situations far
longer than most men would. Women put themselves out there,
wearing their full hearts on their sleeves, forever trusting. I
know too many stories of women in long distance relationships
who faithfully and patiently kept vigil for a boyfriend who was
away in college and who did not come back to them…Wasted
years of emotional energy waiting for a phone call or a weekend
together; energy that should have been directed towards life
experiences and self-growth. Back then, there was also a worst
case scenario, compounded by the social pressure that was
common at the time, where a woman got married because she
was of a certain age, had been with a boyfriend for a long time
and it was "the right thing to do." Unfortunately, these young
women made a life commitment without any emotional probing
of themselves and their connection to the men in question and
their marriages were doomed to failure.

My grandmother seemed to like Konstantin, frequently
extending invitations for lunch and dinner at the apartment.
Behind closed doors, she said things like, "He is only using you,
like a bottle of Coca-Cola. You are a receptacle, a receptacle that
he uses to relieve himself. Or, "You are far too short for him."
Or, "It is a real miracle that you actually have a man interested
in you." Her words struck deep. Many years passed before I
could convince myself that this was not my grandmother talking
but her disease, before I could accept that I was worthy of a
man's genuine interest.

Demented or not, her cruelty became second only to my
mother's. Going home after a date became an ordeal. I tried to
open the bedroom door without making a noise, in complete
dark, lest she wake up from her snoring sleep. Sometimes, I

stayed up in the kitchen until she came out looking for me. I told her I had been home for hours. Other times I kept a nightgown hidden in the kitchen, changing when I arrived home. Such maneuvers often spared me from the litany of insults and offenses that threatened to greet me every time I went out.

My grandmother's dementia squandered the family finances. Over the course of her illness, we hired several caretakers in the form of private nurses, nurses' aides, retired secretaries, and ordinary maids. Almost all of them took advantage of my grandmother sooner or later. Whenever they drove her to the hairdresser, which my grandmother would visit two, sometimes three times a week, the bill included their own coloring, cut and style, along with manicures and pedicures. When they went to the small grocery store around the corner to buy milk and bread, the bill had also included cigarettes and sanitary towels for themselves. I particularly remember Yolanda, an Indian woman from Peru, who supposedly was a retired nurse and was hired as a lady-in-waiting for my grandmother. Having come home one day to find my grandmother crying in the kitchen because Yolanda was refusing to take her to the hairdresser's that morning.

I confronted her. "Yolanda, why aren't you at the hairdresser's? Gloria (the family's hairdresser) must be worried you haven't arrived." I was speechless at her reply.

"Senorita, it's better if we go tomorrow because I am due to have my hair done then. I figured the two of us could go tomorrow and kill two birds with one stone." I fired her on the spot, relying on the maid to take care of my grandmother and keep her company until a new companion could be found.

There were bigger and more dangerous leeches during my grandmother's last years. She decided to become an entrepreneur. Moved by pity for his old mother, my uncle, who controlled the family finances since the death of my grandfather, allowed it. My uncle had not taken into consideration that he lived two hours away and that keeping a close eye on my grandmother's frequent outings to the bank and her frenetic check-writing would prove difficult, if not impossible.

The project that my grandmother had in mind involved starting a small industrial business that would employ several people of dubious origin, never mind the product they were supposed to produce. First, she rented a two-story place, the "factory," where she housed all these "employees." Their job was to design and make comforter sets for the bedroom. Needless to say, not one comforter was ever made, let alone sold. Thousands of bolivars, the Venezuelan currency at the time, were invested into the factory every month, and every month, thousands of bolivars went unaccounted for. The factory became the last repository of the money my grandfather had left, swallowing a small fortune in a short time. The money vanished as if set on fire.

The only thing that could be ascertained was that the trips to Europe taken seasonally by some of the employees and their families were all paid for by my grandmother. One of the employees, Orfidia, a fat, middle-aged-woman with two children and a parrot, had a sister who was a nun. Every time my grandmother paid a visit to the factory, the nun was there. Given that my grandmother had a well-known weakness for priests and nuns and religious folks of all sorts, Orfidia was using her sister to charm my grandmother into paying for more trips and more gifts for herself, her sister, and her two children. My grandmother paid for guitar lessons for one of Orfidia's children, for doctor visits for Orfidia, and for all the food they ate.

Mother's Day lunch, Easter lunch, numerous birthday lunches and of course, Christmas and New Year's lunch, all were celebrated with all the factory employees at the most expensive restaurants in Caracas, all paid for by my grandmother. She even took them to stay with her at the Beach Club. My poor brother attended all those lunches and also stayed at the beach club with them. I refused to be a part of that.

In the meantime, my brother and I had almost no clothes in our closets. My grandmother no longer took me shopping for colorful taffeta dresses and velour gowns. My aunt, my uncle's wife, a sweet and pretty woman, took pity on us, taking us shopping for shoes and clothes.

***

Where was my father through all of this? I think of Yeames' painting, *And when did you last see your father?* which depicts the son of a Royalist being questioned about his missing father, in hiding during the English Civil War. I loved the wax rendition based on the painting that I had seen at Madame Tussaud's wax museum in London when I was eleven. The truth is that we had seen little of my father since our return from Europe. We knew he had eventually married his lover, a Polish lawyer, and that she had bore him two children, our half-sisters. We knew that he held memberships or partnerships at the two most prestigious private hospitals in Caracas, the Hospital de Clinicas Caracas and the Clinica Metropolitana. We also knew he had a lot of money overseas, as the unexpected finding of the account in the South of Spain had attested. We saw him socially, as we would run into him at weddings and social events with my grandmother. It was very hard to see him, dressed to the nines with his new family, drinking and laughing. Once I approached him at one of those millionaire weddings. I wanted to talk to him about studying medicine, about becoming an anesthesiologist, like him. He brusquely rejected the subject, calling my attention instead, to my baby half-sister who lay asleep in her posh baby carriage.

"Papa," I said. "Papa, it's so good to see you."

He acknowledged my presence with a grunt, which I took as an invitation to continue.

"I am thinking of going into anesthesia, like you," I said, excited. "I am so proud of you! When did you decide you were going to study medicine? What made you choose anesthesia as your specialty?"

I had the biggest grin on my face, as I awaited his answer. He took out a cigarette from the inside of his jacket, flipped the lighter open and failed to light it. I watched as he tried a second time, in silence, and a third, until at last, he touched fire to the tip of his cigarette. The tension rose as he looked up to the sky, blowing smoke both through his mouth and his nostrils. "Look," he finally told me. "I don't think it's a good idea. It is a hard life. Why don't you play with your baby sister while I get another drink?"

The austere and powerful man standing outside the operating room in his scrubs all those years ago, who had inspired my interest in medicine, was no more interested in me than a stranger.

Rumors came to my brother and I of a divorce between my father and the second wife, with another woman in the picture. What we did not imagine was that the new love interest, soon to be the third wife, was the same age as my sister. We also heard that he had set up a business, a line of private transportation, consisting of big buses that carried passengers from downtown Caracas to the coastal area where all the beaches and beach clubs were. We set up a meeting, wanting to see him after all this time. He agreed, so he could show off his new girlfriend.

The meeting took place in the evening, at the central station of his transportation business. He greeted us with a smile and an ephemeral kiss on the cheek. There was no hugging or other displays of affection between a father and his two children, whom he had not seen in years and of whom he knew nothing. My brother immediately took note of our father's designer watch and of the expensive, fashionable shoes on his feet.

"Did you see his watch," he later exclaimed in disbelief, "and his shoes, did you see his shoes?" I could not care less about his watch or his shoes. I was in shock at the way he treated us. All throughout the meeting, he behaved as if we were adult acquaintances of his. There was nothing fatherly or protective in his demeanor. It was as if three adults who had not seen each other for a long time were sharing a drink together. Afterwards, he took us for dinner at a mediocre Mexican restaurant, where his girlfriend, Horttenns, yes, with two T's and two N's, waited.

She made a poor showing, appearing young, plastic and cosmetically blown up. She wore artificially colored contact lenses and I couldn't tell whether the very long thin and stringy very blond (almost white) hair was natural or a wig she had put on that night. She was wearing a red vinyl one-piece bodysuit. I had never seen anything like it in my life. I wondered how a person like my father, who had fallen for someone like my mother, with her impeccable, classy style, could get involved with a woman who wore colored contact lenses and red vinyl suits. She acted shy and coy as he told the story of how they had met, how they had slept apart for a long time, especially when they had been visiting her family in the rural town where her mother lived. During the visit, she had stayed with her mother at her childhood home while he had stayed alone in a hotel.

We did not know what to say. Were we supposed to celebrate their candor? Become their accomplices? My brother and I looked at each other and changed the subject. I had asked him about his two children from his second marriage. He had two girls by the Polish lawyer. He did not like the subject. It put a scowl on his face. He said they were fine, that he didn't get to see them much. I thought to myself, another set of fatherless children, another set of children who would suffer a lack of backbone and self-esteem in their lives. He mentioned that we had yet another sibling, a boy, borne by his bride-to-be. They would eventually get married. None of us were invited.

The alleged son looked nothing like my father. My aunts reported that that boy was in fact not my father's, that she had already had him when she met my father. All we knew for sure is that my father would have never named one of his children "Wilmer." Eventually, out of embarrassment, I think, my father would have his own name added to the boy's, and everyone called him by my father's name. Our fruitless meeting came to an end, all of us departing as polite, distant strangers; my brother and I crying painful tears in the car on our way home, afterwards.

One night a few months after this enlightening meeting, my brother was driving around the neighborhood. Out of nowhere a car came straight at him. The driver was completely drunk, going the wrong way, very fast. My brother barely had time to react. He threw himself over to the other side of the passenger compartment, lowering his body as much as he was able to, in an effort to avoid what he had gauged, in the instant before the other car hit him, as a fatal, frontal assault. He survived, miraculously untouched. The car was totaled, and the drunk driver was rushed to a nearby hospital.

I was with my brother the next day when he called my father to tell him about the car and to ask for help paying for repairs. My father said he couldn't give an answer then, that he would have one the following day. He said he would call back and instructed my brother to wait for his call. Almost all of the following day went by and my brother's unease and anxiety grew by the minute, as the phone did not ring.

At seven in the evening, my father finally called. The call was not to commiserate with the terrible experience, or to fulfill his duties as a father, but to dictate terms, as a manager does with an employee, or a king with a subject. He would, my father said, pay for one half of the repair of the totaled car, in two parts.

The sadness in my brother's eyes when he hung up the phone broke my heart. He was going to have to ask my uncle for the rest of the money, even though his own father could easily have paid for the repairs with no real pinch to his bank account or standard of living. I felt for my brother, as I had often felt for myself.

***

In spite of our home situation, the lack of support or encouragement from either parent, my brother and I remained committed to our studies. We continued to be excellent students and pleasant, well-behaved adolescents. The same could not be said about my sister. She never finished her philosophy degree at the university. She had more contact with our father, and he offered to pay for a degree in programming. To this day, I don't know whose idea it was that computer programming was an option for her. She had often said the thought of computer programming, or anything that required the kind of abstract thinking that "being good at math" had implied, made her break into a sweat. She quit after the first week. Next, she enrolled at some academy for decorating and design. She liked this better, attended regularly, which brought a sense of order and decorum to her life.

By then, my mother had been gone for three years. She had left when I was thirteen and my brother eleven. I thought I felt fine without her, thought myself unbeatable, powerful. Only in the years to come would I realize that her absence kept the wound of my parent's divorce open, preventing it from healing.

Trauma can fester unseen, much like a cancer detected all too late.

Light Seeps In

The summer I was sixteen, my mother and my grandmother decided it was time for my brother and I to pay a visit to the United States. We were to travel to the state of Virginia, where my mother had settled with her second husband. My grandmother bought us tickets and gave us a little spending money for the trip. My brother and I agreed to go to my mother on the condition that my mother would promise us on the phone that under no circumstance was she to lay a finger on us. There must be an understanding that if she touched us again, if she hit us, we would hit back. I personally wanted to slap her and break her face like she had done to me so many times in the past. My mother swore on her father's eternal rest that she would never touch us again. To everyone's surprise she kept her promise.

The two summers we spent in Virginia were the closest to a normal family life any of us ever knew together. My stepfather never quite finished the law degree he had set out to pursue in Cuba. Instead, upon arriving in the United States, his focus turned to business. After several failed ventures, including a Cuban restaurant, he became a used car salesman. He actually did very well at the used car dealership, where he managed to be the recipient of "salesman of the month" and "salesman of the year" awards on numerous occasions. The little bit of money left over after paying the bills he gladly spent on us. Once, I bought a pair of jeans, worn them once and decided I did not like how they fit. The following morning when I woke up, he had already washed my jeans, ironed them and was in the process of sewing back the tags so that I could return them at the store. He had also fished for the receipt in the trash.

As for my mother, she worked at a private Catholic school teaching Spanish literature to high schoolers. She excelled at it. Word of my mother's talent quickly spread and for many of her working years, she was invited to be a reader at college entrance examinations for students of Spanish and Spanish literature. Teaching was the best thing that ever happened to my mother. Working stabilized her. It had a calming effect on her. For the first time in her life, she felt useful. She had a routine. She was able to get up in the morning and go to work. The home that my stepfather provided for her and for us, was the closest thing to a normal family life we had ever experienced. They seemed happy with their lot in life. They cherished one another and seemed very much in love. He was able to control her outbursts, providing her with a sense of balance and solidity.

It was also a time of stability for my brother and me. For the very first time in our lives, the children could behave as children because the adults behaved like adults. My stepfather initiated the legal process to claim us as his children in order to get us residency permits and legalize us in the United States. I will never be able to repay him for doing so. The ages of sixteen and seventeen were the happiest two years of my life, up to that point, thanks to him. I loved spending time with my engineer, pole-vaulter American boyfriend, I had some friends at school. I spent the summers with my mother and my stepfather, and my application for a green card was being processed. I became a runner and committed myself to physical fitness for life. The same discipline that had so served me academically, I applied to running and climbing up the hills of several parks in our city. I credit my athletic boyfriend with introducing me to athletics. I learned to run by running behind him, panting, spitting and swearing. But in the end, I did learn. Being active and maintaining my physical fitness would provide psychological therapy to avoid major depression and major mood changes in my life.

I was sixteen when I was accepted into medical school. Usually, high school graduates were required to wait for one year, but the university made an exception for a small group of applicants to start right away. There were no years spent on undergraduate, pre-med study. At that time in Venezuela, young people were expected to know at seventeen their final career choice. As for tuition, the Universidad Central de Venezuela trained me to become a physician at no cost. There are not enough words in any language to express my eternal gratitude to the Maxima Casa de Estudios, as our glorious university is also known, for the opportunity to fulfill my childhood dream of becoming a doctor and doing something useful with my life. Had the tuition not been free, I would have never been able to attend medical school, as the factory had drained all the money my grandfather left when he died and my father was fiscally unaccountable.

I turned seventeen in April and graduated from high school in June. To this day, I treasure my high school graduation ceremony in spite of my parents' absence. Only my grandmother attended. For the occasion, my grandmother bought me a beautiful morning dress in salmon pink, with rosy beige shoes and a purse to match. The ceremony was perfect, not too long, not too short. The director of the school gave a speech with a message that resonated with me: We were to go out into the world to serve others and make a difference. I felt ready, my heart bursting with compassion, eager to help others through the practice of medicine, to alleviate pain, and to give hope. My high school graduation was the very first milestone on the path to my dream, and I graduated with honors. I felt happy, proud.

That night, the entire group of graduating girls went to a club that was part of the most fashionable restaurant in town. We all brought our boyfriends or dates. My boyfriend looked sharp in his navy blue suit and his striped red tie. I wore a new dress, also in navy blue, in the most delicate brocade, with high-heeled pumps that my grandmother's seamstress had carefully covered with a blue lining in to match the exact shade of my dress. I had gone to the hairdressers that day and my hair was beautifully set. As for my jewelry, I borrowed the most elegant set of pearl earrings and necklace from my grandmother. The small gestures of love I received from my grandmother filled up my emotional tank for some years to come. As a child of my parents, I was used to emotionally running on very little, an emotional tank that was permanently almost empty. I had adapted, managing an efficient economy. It was not yet time for me to realize it didn't have to be that way, that such an impoverished emotional life was not the norm.

In spite of the celebration and festivities surrounding my graduation, I faced the problem of not having a car in which to drive myself to medical school. I decided to gather up my courage and contact my father. I was going to present my case, sure that I would win. After all, I was following in his footsteps. It took several phone calls and pages to get a hold of him. He seemed to be avoiding me. I will never know why. I have learnt not to waste too much time trying to understand the reasons someone who was supposed to be my parent refused to help me, could not even find the time to speak with me.

Eventually I reached my father.

"I can only afford to buy you a basic stick shift model," he said, adding, "without air-conditioning."

"You are going to let me attend medical school in a car with no air-conditioning, despite the infernal tropical heat?"

"It is what I can afford."

"Remind me, Father. Does your mistress drive a BMW and your wife a Mercedes? Or is it the other way around."

"Take what I give you and be grateful. Or not."

I could tell by the sound of his voice that he was about to hang up the phone.

"I'll take it!" I shouted. "Thank you. Thank you, very much."

Immediately I phoned my uncle, who worked in the car business and had contacts at several dealerships. It was because of my uncle's diligence and interest in me, and yes, thanks to my mother, who had been working as a teacher and had managed to save one thousand dollars to send to me, that I was soon able to trade in the car that my father bought for me for a better model —one that came with air-conditioning.

With the transportation issue solved, I felt unstoppable. Around the time I finally started medical school, I began to notice a veritable demonstration of "ask and you shall receive." In spite of the difficulties in my life, I was always provided, in one way or another, the things that really mattered, the ones that would bring growth and improvement. Often these blessings arrived through unforeseen or unexpected channels. That important realization affirmed my faith in God, in life, and strengthened the hope that would push me and guide me through life. Through the trying years of medical school, my faith and trust in life never let me lose sight of my goal.

***

My stepfather loved road trips. He loved listening to Cuban music in the car and eating at fast food places on the highway stops. He was particularly fond of Popeyes. Even I came to enjoy the crispy fried chicken and mashed potatoes. He drove us to Williamsburg, the colonial town in Eastern Virginia, that depicted life during the eighteenth century, when it had been the state capital. On another trip, he took us to a Catholic sanctuary, the shrine of Mother Elizabeth Seaton, in Emmetsburg, Maryland. Mother Seton had been the first native-born American saint recognized by the Roman Catholic Church. My stepfather was a deeply religious man who would pray the rosary every day and was particularly devoted to the Virgin Mary. A lot of the choices for our road trips were influence by the mandates of the Catholic Church and the canonized or beatified people it revered.

Even though things would not always be perfect between my stepfather and me, the summer of my high school graduation he gave me a wonderful gift. My brother was included in the gift because his high school graduation would take place the following year, as he had skipped a year of school when he returned from England. Our graduation gift was the road trip of a lifetime. My stepfather took us to New York City, with a stop in Atlantic City, New Jersey, to give us a taste of the casinos and the gambling life. My brother and I had never seen anything like it: the lights, the sounds, the people, old, and young, rich, poor. In New York we lost our way on the subway. For the first time in my life, I did not care that we were lost. I could have sat in those subway cars forever, people watching, taking it all in. It was a wonderful, unforgettable graduation gift, our road trip to New York. My stepfather was no doubt a giver. Back home from the road trip, he made a meal of garlic sautéed shrimp for us. He prepared that shrimp to perfection. He had the gift of making everything look effortlessly simple, easy.

My stepfather was heedless of his health. He smoked a lot and was not careful about what he put in his mouth. He frequently ate at McDonald's, and all of the combo meals he ordered had included a super-sized, sugar- and fat-loaded vanilla milkshake. He was stubborn and obstinate about doing things his way. The only religion that was true and worthy of following, for example, was his religion. Every other day or so, he would sit me down and read passages out of the Bible. He made me pray the rosary with him. He woke up very early in the morning, went to mass and stayed at the church to venerate and keep guard at the

"Blessed Sacrament," the blood and body of Christ in the form of consecrated bread and wine.

Even after my stepfather survived a massive heart attack, he continued to drink his vanilla milkshakes. The very night of his infarction he lit up a cigarette to see if his chest pain would subside. My mother was hysterical, telling him the pressure he felt on his chest was a heart attack, to please put out the cigarette and let her drive him to the hospital right away. He refused. In despair, my mother called the paramedics. The delay in receiving the appropriate treatment, in the form of an angioplasty and a stent, had dire consequences. His heart function declined by a third. It was his right coronary artery that had been blocked, causing not only necrosis and death of precious cardiac muscle, but damage to the pacemaker cells in his heart. He never really took care of his heart, developing a dilated cardiomyopathy and necessitating a pacemaker and eventually a defibrillator to prevent sudden death from malignant arrhythmias.

My stepfather also developed diabetes, and very early after his diagnosis required shots of insulin. His very difficult-to-treat blood sugar levels would lead to numerous coronary interventions and stent deployments over the years. He gained a lot of weight, suffered very bad osteoarthritis in his knees, and continued to smoke for a while after his coronary event, though he did eventually give up the habit. He took care of things whenever he was ready, no matter how pressing they might be, and not a moment before. It was just his way.

Whenever friends or family visited Miami, he insisted on having guava pastries sent over to Virginia, where they lived, from Miami via courier. I refused to contribute to the detriment of his already very poor health. After he had completed his cardiac rehabilitation, I bought a treadmill for him, and to my surprise he had actually used it and did not gain any more weight.

Unbeknownst to me, my stepfather came into the marriage to my mother carrying a lot of debt. He had been irresponsible not only in the way lived his life, not taking care of his health, but also in the way he sometimes chose to spend money. My uncle, God bless him, had the generosity and the heart to help my mother and my stepfather alleviate what had become "their" accrued debt by marriage. Once, during the years that my uncle worked as an executive for an American company in Paris, France, he flew my mother and stepfather over, paying all of their expenses during the stay.

The visit did not go well, however. My stepfather, my aunt, and my uncle were each victims of my mother's wrath. They all stayed at my uncle's apartment, on Paris's elegant sixteenth arrondissement. My uncle and my aunt were excited to be able to provide a break of such magnitude for my stepfather and my mother, in the form of a two weeks in Paris. Things started to sour when my mother decided she didn't want to go out into the city. She had no interest in sightseeing or investigating the latest exhibits at the museums. No, she only wanted to leave my uncle's apartment to go to the most expensive a la mode restaurants. When my uncle had refused to dine out every single night because he enjoyed my aunt's cooking, and it would also be outrageously expensive, my mother threw a fit, and to my uncle's dismay, my stepfather backed my mother up unconditionally. It was as if he felt the relentless need to prove his love for my mother at all times.

My mother proceeded to use the house phone to contact every one of her friends and acquaintances in Europe, all the way from Switzerland to Spain. She was on the phone for hours. My uncle and several others tried to call the house, always getting a busy signal. When my uncle brought her abuse of their phone to her attention, she simply ignored his plea. The phone bill that month was astronomical. Any thoughtful human being, any person with an ounce of decency, would have offered to pay the phone bill, if not in its entirety, at least for a portion of it. She did not. My uncle had given her some spending money and she could have given it back to him to help pay the phone bill, but she did not do that, either. She chose instead to spend it on compact discs and cassette tapes at the local music store. Her musical bounty would not even fit in her suitcase.

My uncle went out and bought a second suitcase for her, but it was not mere generosity. He had discovered my mother's real intentions; she had planned to stay in France, not returning to the United States, ever. She announced her intention matter-of-factly, as if my uncle were obligated to satisfy all of her whims and demands. She couldn't stay, of course, not least because she had taken an unfounded, unrealistic animosity towards my aunt, directing all her hatred and frustration in life towards her. My aunt was innocent. She had done nothing to provoke my mother's hatred. If anything, she had gone out of her way to buy clothes and shoes for my brother and for me and had invited us to stay at their house in Valencia, Venezuela, the city where they lived before moving to France.

One night, in Paris, the four of them went out to dinner and were riding back home in a taxi. A conversation between my mother and my aunt quickly spiraled out of control. My mother jumped out of the car and threw herself at another taxicab, screaming: "Help! Help! My own brother wants to hurt me. Help me!" The incident ended at the local police department. I can only imagine my uncle's sadness and despair. As for my mother, she must have been at the zenith of what she knew how to do best: create suffering for herself and for others. Instead of calming my mother down, my stepfather joined her in accusations about my uncle stealing the inheritance that my grandfather had left her. Nothing had been further from the truth.

***

When my mother and my stepfather returned to the United States with an extra suitcase full of compact discs and poetry books it was to their compact apartment, what she liked to refer to as "two bedrooms and one corridor." There, they resumed what had become a life of loneliness in their togetherness. They rarely went out or saw anyone else other than the people at church (him), or the cat (her). Before their self-imposed confinement, before he got really sick, while they were still an active part of the working world, my brother moved in with them. He had to wait for twelve months, by custom, before starting medical school. During that time, my stepfather became the closest thing to a father my brother ever had. My brother was sixteen, old enough to hold two jobs, one at the local gas station, the other one at McDonald's. It must have been an exhilarating experience, to make money, to derive a paycheck at such an early age. In Venezuela, teenagers did not work.

***

In the last three weeks before I was to start medical school at the university, the thought occurred to me that perhaps my father had wanted to give me a graduation present and he had simply not had the chance to do so. A partner had two private clinics; my father was earning considerable amounts of money. He owned properties abroad, one apartment in Paris and another one in the south of Spain. I had the brilliant idea to ask my father if my best friend and I could spend five days, perhaps a week, in his apartment in the south of Spain, in Marbella, as a graduation gift. Marbella was the jet-set vacationing place where my mother had discovered one of his secret bank accounts.

"No," he said forcefully. "Absolutely not."

"Why?" I asked, unable to hide my disappointment and sadness.

"First," he began, as though explaining a business matter to a patient, "the apartment has already been rented out for a year."

He thought for a moment, and before I could speak, he went on.

"How will you afford your airline ticket? You have no money! You have no conception of money! Do you know how much a cup of coffee costs in Spain? Sixty bolivars! That is a fortune for you. You don't even have enough to buy a cup of coffee in Venezuela."

"I can do without coffee," I retorted, but my voice sounded weak in my own ears. I could not believe he could be so miserly and cruel. I was defeated. At last I knew to expect nothing, ever, from my father.

"Never mind," I said. "It was just an idea."

I did my best not to dwell on my father and this disappointment.

I started medical school in the fall. I was seventeen years old and still sleeping in my grandmother's room. I coveted my sister's room, which she locked every time she would go out so I couldn't borrow any of her clothes. I remember that once or twice, the maid, who kept a set of keys to my sister's room in order to clean it, had let me inside, to borrow something to wear for a party. What I had seen inside I would never see again in my life. Layers, drifts, dunes of clothing—dresses, shirts, shorts, beach towels, handbags, trousers, shoes–covered the entire floor. I had to step on her clothes to get to the closet. Among the clothes still hanging in the closet, I found something nice to wear.

During my high school years, the maid, Nivia, and I grew close. She was a Colombian woman, in her thirties, which seemed an advance age to me then, energetic, hard-working, very clean and very upbeat. She was a heavy smoker. I did not mind her habit. The scent of the cigarette smoke had a soothing effect on me. She was very kind to my brother and me. Perhaps because she saw my grandmother's rapid decline into dementia, she knew we had nobody else to take care of us. Because of her, I learned to be open minded and open hearted about receiving affection and love.

If this maid was exceptional, her predecessor was a nightmare. She was a young girl from the Venezuelan countryside. During the eight months she was with us, Maribel managed to fool us all. She prepared coconut desserts and other sweet concoctions that appealed to my grandmother's sweet tooth. She sang religious hymns with my grandmother and prayed the rosary with her. In the meantime, she and my grandmother's driver schemed to rob our apartment. She waited for a weekend when my grandmother visited her sister, many miles away. My brother was over at some friend's house, and I was at the beach club for the weekend.

I left Friday for the beach club, by myself, for a weekend of relaxation and tanning. In those days, the strangest, most exotic concoctions were mixed up to serve as tan accelerators. Coca-Cola, cinnamon and Mennen baby oil for example, were a staple in my beach bag. "Maribel!" I called out as I walked into the kitchen. Miguel, the driver, was there next to her. Both stood very still , as if caught in the middle of something.

"Maribel! Didn't you hear me call you? Where is the Coca-Cola I asked you for?"

I was met with a blank stare.

"Did the cat eat your tongue? Are you ok?"

"Yes, yes, I'm sorry Senorita" she said. "I was thinking of the festivities in my hometown for the Virgin of Coromoto. Did you know I am very devout?" Before I got a chance to answer she handed me the soft drink.

"Here is your Coca-Cola, Senorita."

All morning I harbored an unsettled feeling, a dark suspicion that Maribel and the driver were accomplices in some mischief.

Under the force of this impression, I felt more alone than ever. Used to dealing with anxiety, I dismissed the dreadful thought. I filled up my mind with images of the beach, coconut shakes, and my tan. Off I went with a smile.

Saturday morning was glorious, not one cloud in the blue tropical skies, which initially made me doubt the weather forecast for the afternoon. Heavy rains were expected to start at around 4 p.m. I felt a tinge of anxiety; wondering if my boyfriend who was in Mexico City for a few days at an athletic meet, had called the apartment and I had missed it. I called the apartment from a public phone. The phone rang and rang. No one picked up. This is strange, I thought to myself. Maribel is supposed to be there. Forty-five minutes later I called again. No answer. Maybe she went to the bread store, the panaderia around the corner.

At three p.m. I called again. This time she picked up on the first ring.

"Where were you? Why didn't you answer the phone?"

"Oh, I was asleep." She did not sound asleep.

"Whatever. Has my boyfriend called?"

"No, Senorita, he has not. By the way Senorita, when are you coming home?"

"I was thinking of leaving now."

I heard her take a deep, sharp breath.

"Senorita, there is no need to come now. Come home tomorrow. Your boyfriend never calls in the evenings when he travels. I am sure he will ring you tomorrow during the day. Do stay at the beach and enjoy your time."

"Ok, see you tomorrow," I said with a shrug, hanging up the phone.

Instead, I carried my bag to the car and started driving home. I can't remember why I decided to come home a day early, but once I fixated on a plan there was no deterring me. The storm did hit as predicted. The streets were flooded. I drove a stick shift Fiat and it was not long before the engine got wet and the car stopped running. I put it in neutral and pushed it to the side of the road. The rain kept falling, and I knew it wouldn't stop for several hours. I ended up spending the night in the back of my car, sleeping the peaceful sleep of the innocents, feeling protected by the torrential rain that I was sure deterred any assailants. At 3 a.m. the rain finally stopped. At 4 a.m. my car started. I made it home safely and triumphantly unprepared for what came next.

I opened the door to the apartment and found my grandmother's TV set standing in the middle of the living room. That was odd, but in my naivety, I thought nothing of it. I walked around it to my bedroom and opened my closet to choose an outfit to wear to my good friend Kirsten's birthday party. To my dismay, the closet was bare. Everything was gone. Maribel had taken everything, including all of my brother's clothes. With the help of the chauffeur, she had packed it all into my grandmother's car, and driven away in the middle of the night. I went to check Maribel's own closet in the maid's room and everything was gone too. To this day, the thought of her causes distress and anger. My grandmother was livid, still able to grasp the colossal loss. Luckily for all of us, my uncle put on his black shining armor and like a brave, generous knight, bought her a new car and a new TV set. As for our clothes, in the only act of compassion of his whole life, albeit reluctantly, my father gave us the equivalent of two hundred and fifty US dollars each.

***

My sister disappeared for one more trip, one last incognito expedition around the Venezuelan countryside. She decided to abandon her studies at the design academy to provide companionship to a male friend who travelled around the country distributing illegal substances. There were two additional travelers in the group: an Asian woman and her little baby. Around and around they went in a beat up old car. Why did my sister do this? What did she need in her life that made her pack up and leave my grandmother's apartment where she at least had a room to herself, food, and a maid to clean her room and wash her clothes? In the end, my mother came to the rescue. In the only act of motherly love towards my sister—the only one in her entire life—she took her to live with her in Virginia. My uncle paid for my sister to attend a local junior college. She thrived under the influence of my stepfather, until, two months short of graduation, she quit.

But patterns can be difficult to erase. She never graduated from college. She never finished anything. Like her mother, she married a man whom she had known for barely two weeks.

Adversities Become Gifts

With my sister away, I had my own room. I had my privacy. I could arrive after ten in the evening without fear of insults and humiliations. I had my own room, I had a kind, caring maid who cooked my meals, washed my clothes and cleaned my room. I had a car. I was in medical school and I was already excelling at it. I was happy.

Luckily, I lived very close to campus, so my driving time was ten minutes, at most. This felt like a great reward. During all my school years in Venezuela, I rode the school bus for two hours in the morning. The elementary school years were the hardest. We were still at the Big House, and we would have to wake up at six to be ready and out the door by six-twenty as the bus stopped for exactly ninety seconds in front of the house, If the driver detected no movement (lights being turned on, an open front door) he wouldn't wait at all. My grandmother dressed me in the mornings, while I was still asleep in bed. I remember how she gently moved my limbs out of the pajamas, and softly bent them and manipulated them around and into the school uniform.

I knew then that it was time to wake up and get ready for school, but my eyelids were so very heavy, and my mind wanted to dwell in slumbers, where the dreamscape was that of small, wild, forest animals, squirrels, raccoons, rabbits, that lay curled up, dormant inside the holes of massive tree trunks, hibernating for the winter. Very slowly, the scene would become blurry, the picture losing its crispness and clarity…And then I was awake. The soothing winter dream-quality lingered for the seven minutes I had to eat breakfast in my "Peter Rabbit" dishware. To this day, I call upon my childhood winter imagery to help me fall asleep.

Once on the school bus, I looked out the window for the next twenty minutes, searching for stray dogs on the street. Caracas was full of stray dogs. I was captivated by their mauled, skeletal bodies, their fur, dirty and discolored, and the sad, hopeless look of chronic starvation in their sunken eyes. The bitches ambulated slowly and furtively, their hypertrophied mammary glands dragging the ground, their malnourished puppies hidden in some foul-smelling alley...hopeless bitches that still did everything in their power to care for their litters; in sharp contrast with humans who cast off so easily those in their care. I could not look away from these miserable creatures, crying silently for their plight, until my eyes grew heavy and my head leaned against the window, and I dreamed again of squirrels, raccoons and rabbits nestled safe within the massive trunks of trees.

It was always uncomfortable to wake up, disoriented and groggy, to the laughter and the screaming of the other children in the bus. It was almost painful to walk off the bus carrying the backpack, heavy with books, notebooks and pads. My fascination with the street curs did not last into high school. By then, I rarely looked out the window at all, and never dozed with my head against it. Instead, I studied the material for whatever test or exam I happened to have that day. The other girls called me a nerd and stopped including me in their gossipy conversations. I did not care. I thought myself lucky to live far away from school, to have the gift of two additional hours of study and review as the bus made its rounds, picking up students.

Now, as I began medical school, I knew that the ability to turn perceived adversity into advantage was one of my strengths. I turned my mind and my energy toward new difficulties and how they could be made to become gifts.

***

For five months, my cute little car worked perfectly, consumed little gas, and was a pleasure to drive. One Monday morning, the car refused to start. I turned the key in the ignition, over and over, pushed on the pedal, did not push on the pedal, changed gears back and forth. Nothing. I sat in the car for a few minutes, figuring what my next plan would be. I could try to borrow my grandmother's new car. I could call a taxi. I had no friends that lived close by to give me a lift. I felt my face redden, as every minute that went by meant I was getting closer and closer to being late for anatomy lab.

Finally, I gave it one more desperate try. To my surprise, this time it worked. The engine started. Grateful and relieved, I drove happily to school. The following morning, the engine started effortlessly at one turn of the key. I thought myself set for life. Wednesday morning, the engine failed to start. I tried the same maneuvers I had tried on Monday. I was able to start the car, but not before trying for twenty-five minutes.

As I pulled into the parking lot, I debated whether I should call my father or not. I decided to page him and tell him about the unpredictability of my car. I paged him again at noon. I paged one last time in the late afternoon. Miraculously, the following morning, the engine decided to start without fuss. I paged my father again, just in case. No reply. My father never called me back and I knew he was not traveling.

Faced with the anxiety of being late for class, I devised the following plan: I would set my alarm clock to go off an hour earlier in the morning. I would get ready as usual and then venture into the garage to cajole the delicate engine into turning over. Sometimes it would start after two tries with the key, other times it could take as long as thirty minutes.

Until the morning when it did not start at all. I had to go back upstairs to the apartment, call a taxi, and then, arming myself with patience, go back downstairs to the entrance of the building to wait for the taxi to take me to medical school. The prospect of being late filled me with anxiety—and worse was yet to come. I agonized about having to call my father again, about being rejected, about how on earth was I going to get the money to tow the car to the shop, and for whatever repairs were needed.

That morning, as I stood in front of my building waiting for the taxi, I made a promise. I swore to myself that once I finished medical school, I would never ask anybody for money for anything, ever. Especially men. I vowed to be completely independent, financially and emotionally, always. I never wanted to be subjected again to neglect and rejection by the men who were supposed to care about me.

That, however, was the future. I needed help, now. The next morning, I showed up in person at the clinic where my father was seeing cases that day. He had been terribly busy, he said, and unable to return three days of my phone calls. I did not waste time scoffing at this pitiless explanation or on trying to get an apology. I simply and plainly told him that I needed for him to arrange to tow my car to the repair shop to get checked by a mechanic. For once, he acceded, calling one of his mechanic friends to pick the car and look at it. In the meantime, I called a taxi every time I had needed to go anywhere.

To this day I don't know exactly what had been wrong with the car. I do remember, however, my father trying to get me to pay for half of the repair bill. We were discussing the matter on the telephone.

"How can I pay for this if I do not have an income? I don't work, and medical school is a full-time job!" I said.

A protracted silence ensued over the phone, until he said, "Make your mother pay for it."

"As you well know, my mother is working as a teacher in the United States because her husband has no money."

"Your grandmother then." His coldness took my breath.

"I think you should pay for the repairs," I said through tears, voice quavering. "You are my father. I need to go to school, graduate, and get a job so I will never, ever ask you for anything ever again."

He remained silent. I gathered my courage. Wiping my eyes with the heel of my hand, I said, "It is in your best interest to pay for my car. It is the way for you to be rid of me, once and for all. That's what you want, isn't it?"

I could hear his breathing through the telephone line. Otherwise, I might have thought he had hung up.

"All right," he said. "All right. Have the bill sent to me."

It was the outcome I needed but still devastating to accept the reality of his indifference.

***

I enjoyed medical school despite the workload. At the end of the first year, I received an award for academic excellence. I also developed an athletic routine, if one may call it that. Whenever I had a (relatively) short day, I would join my pole-vaulter boyfriend at his university campus. Together we would jog along the beautiful, green, hilly campus. It had been there, under his supervision, that I discovered my athletic endurance. On the weekends, I enjoyed the "subidas de cerro," hiking on the trails of our national park, up the Avila mountain range, right outside Caracas. It was a beautiful city in those days. The Avila had several entrances, one a mere two miles from my house. On both weekend mornings I would take off early and hike up to the "cortafuego," a flat area of terrain where I would go running after the hike. The hike took twenty minutes, and I ran for thirty. It felt great. The mixture of perfect weather, not too hot because it was still early in the morning, and the backdrop of the majestic Avila Mountains was unbeatable.

Used to hiking alone I gave no thought to safety despite the disturbios, the riots that had become a frequent occurrence in those years. Commander Hugo Chavez was trying to make a name for himself, accusing and condemning the two major political parties of corruption and misuse of funds. He wanted to portray himself as the savior of the innocent masses, promising to be an honest, fair leader, an honorable president. After a failed coup d'état and a stint in prison, he was released and founded a political party that promised transparency and fresh, new ideologies. He struck a chord with the majority of the people, everybody being tired of money disappearing, and of political favoritism.

Chavez won the presidential election with the support of practically the entire population. The disturbios, which mobilized thousands of people living up on the mountains, in the shanty-towns, were a real reason to be afraid. The crowds would break into supermarkets, stores of all sorts, and steal not only food, but electronics, furniture—whatever they could get their hands on. In high school, I remember partaking in a charity that helped the children of the poor; the Ursuline nuns had set up an elementary school for the disadvantaged. Every Tuesday afternoon, we would take food, clothes and toys to the shantytowns, the barrios, which were the equivalent of the Brazilian favelas.

My protégé was a little boy, Roger, thin as a rail with a big mouth full of the brightest, shiniest teeth. Regretfully, they were all crooked. Like many South American children, myself included, there had never been a father around. He must have been around seven years old. I brought him a hotdog and a bag of potato chips from the food kiosk at my school. He stared hungrily at the food.

"Can I eat it now, Miss?" he asked.

"Of course, I got it for you!"

Roger unwrapped the hotdog and broke it in half, wrapping one of the halves and putting it in his torn backpack. He did not open the bag of chips.

"Roger, why don't you eat the rest of the hotdog?"

"I am saving this half for my mother, Miss. She is hungry too, Miss."

He happily chewed on his hotdog, as his friends laughed and played around us.

"When are you coming back to see me, Miss?" he managed to say between small bites.

"Soon Roger, soon" I told him, as I caressed the small, curly head.

And in his innocent and trusting happy-go-lucky ways, he said, "Thank you Miss" and ran off to join his pals, taking a piece of my heart with him. That was the last time I saw him. Soon after it became very dangerous to visit the shantytowns and my high school put a temporary stop to the weekly excursions.

Hungry people protested in the streets. The middle class was on the verge of disappearing. Robberies and violent crime rose by the day. My car got broken into three times in a period of eight months. They broke into my car to steal whatever was on the passenger seat, which were old, worn sweaters that I wore for school. My car was modest. Those who drove expensive cars installed high-caliber alarms and security systems to deter thieves.

No street was safe. As I walked to the grocery store, the "fruteria," around the corner from my apartment building, a teenage boy appeared from nowhere, and started to walk hurriedly on the same sidewalk I was on, in the opposite direction. As we crossed paths, he yanked the crucifix and chain from my neck, and took off running as fast as his feet let him. On another occasion, I was coming down from the Cerro Avila, my morning hike already done, when at the entrance of the national park, a man appeared from behind some bushes. He carried a knife, swinging it from side to side.

"Give me your watch or I'll kill you."

I wore a plastic watch, a Swiss Watch that was very popular back then. I was also carrying mace. The man got very close.

"No! My boyfriend gave it to me and you will not have it!"

I sprayed the mace on him for a good eight seconds. The man started to cry as he covered his face with his hands. At that moment I realized he could have killed me. I took off, running as fast as I could, screaming on top of my lungs and crying.

In spite of the watch incident, I refused to hand over any jewelry that I happened to be wearing anytime a thief would approach. Several years later, when my mother had temporarily come home from the United States to help put my grand-mother's affairs in order, my brother, my mother and I were waiting for my mother's friend outside his building. The three of us were sitting in my car, with the windows open, the engine off. Out of nowhere, a man stood by the driver's side, leaning into me.

"You guys listen," he said. "It is not my fault that I am a drug addict and I need money to support my habit. I have a gun on me and I have no problem using it on you if you don't hand all your watches over right now."

I had on an eighteen-karat gold Cartier Love bracelet that my grandmother had given me for my eighteenth birthday. As the man spoke, he alternated looking at me and looking around the car and keeping an eye out for policemen. I swiftly pulled the bracelet off my wrist and hid it between my leg and the seat. The man never noticed.

He walked away with my mother's and brother's watches. I wanted to get out of the car and attack him. This isn't to say that I was not without sympathy for the poor people who made up the bulk of the city's population, but I was very angry at this assault. I was sure the villain had not been carrying a gun. I started to open my car door, but my brother begged me to drive to the police station instead.

I told one of the officers that we had just been robbed by a man who claimed to have a gun. The officer eyed me up and down. He had a smirk on his face and he kept winking at me.

"Calmate mami (calm down, love)," he repeated, over and over as he licked his lips.

I felt uncomfortable. I felt he was mocking me, that he had bad intentions and wanted to play around with me. I walked out of the police station, in new awareness of the sad truth: Venezuela had become a no man's land, its citizens abandoned, left to fend for themselves. The police were bribed by the drug dealers, no doubt, protected by a system that prospered on corruption that went all the way to the top—to the Senate, to Congress.

It was the beginning of the end. Assailants waited for victims by hiding under cars that were parked on the street, lurking, at all hours. They hid in ditches on the roads, on the motorways, from which they threw rocks at the passing cars, hoping the driver would stop to check the damage, at which point a crowd would clamber out of hiding to rob and shoot the victim. Even if one handed a wallet, car keys and jewelry, the assailants might still shoot one on a leg, or a foot. It was no longer a question of being hungry or on drugs. A new cancer in the form of social resentment rapidly metastasized. It was the war of the poor against the perceived rich, marked by the invasion of private property and, in later years, by the rationing of food and medicines. The nation slid ever more deeply into ruin.

***

As my twenty-first birthday approached, I was no longer seeing my pole-vaulter. After five years together, we no longer wanted the same things. The relationship died a slow death, and my spirit was overtaken by a fatalism that robbed me of my usual relentless, invincible demeanor. I had nothing to look forward to. Then, a cousin who was getting married in the next few months announced she wanted me to be the maid of honor. Being in that wedding made a huge difference for me. It gave me a sense of anticipation for something other than study and hiking. I felt a part of the family because someone had thought to include me. A little love goes a long way when you've been starved for it since childhood. (Fifteen years later, I learned that my grandmother, sensing my sadness and despair, had begged my cousin to make me her maid of honor, one of those secret acts of love that my grandparents had been so fond of.)

I met my second boyfriend, and future husband, at my cousin's wedding. He was the best man, and for me, it was almost love at first sight. My husband-to-be and the future father of my child made an impression that night. Born to an Aruban father of Dutch ancestry and a Chilean mother of English-Scottish ancestry, he was a well-mannered, soft spoken, perfectly elegant gentleman. He was fluent in four languages and had an international flair. The day of the wedding, I had been waiting at the hairdresser's for my hair and make-up to be done for what seemed an eternity, nervous and excited to meet the best man. Of all the girls in the wedding party, my hair and make-up were done last. As soon as the last stroke of pink blush had gone on my cheeks, I was hurried into one of the bridal cars, together with the other bridesmaids, and was driven to the bride's house.

We were late! Once arrived, I rushed upstairs to change into my maid-of-honor dress. It was a very becoming, off-the-shoulder gown in fuchsia, the taffeta delicately woven together in the front to form one single flower at the cleavage, a rose. My hair was tied up in a low chignon, which drew attention to my collarbone, and from there to my shoulders and on to the gorgeous fuchsia gown. I took one last reassuring look in my cousin's full-length bathroom mirror. I was satisfied. I hurried downstairs to meet the best man, who was pacing anxiously in the living room, waiting to be introduced to his maid-of-honor.

Coming down the spiraled staircase, I caught a glimpse of him, standing in the corner, a champagne flute in his hand, talking to one of the bridesmaids. He was tall, with beautiful auburn hair, and a toothy, pleasant smile. I reached the bottom of the stairs and went to him.

"Hello, I'm Ana Maria, the maid of honor. It's nice to finally meet you."

He looked at me and smiled briefly. I detected a tinge of fakery, of forced politeness that made me uneasy. In spite of the artificial quality of the encounter, in my mind, I decided to give him a chance.

"I am Rusty," he said.

"Rusty!" I said. "Is that your real name? Where are you from, Rusty?"

At this, Rusty relaxed a little. This time, his smile felt more genuine. "I am from Aruba, born in Peru, and my real name is Russell."

"Listen everybody!" the mother of the bride had interrupted. "It's time to go to the church, let's not forget this is a wedding. The limousines are lined up outside."

Rusty put his drink down on one of the side tables and motioned for me to follow him as the level of noise in the house quickly rose. We rode together to the church. He told me he was taken by my English accent. I was taken by his worldliness and by his beautiful auburn hair. During the ride he offered unintelligible phrases in a foreign language that sounded Germanic and I could tell from the dreamy look in his eyes that he was flirting with me. If he had been trying to charm me, he had definitely and unapologetically succeeded.

Quickly I learned Rusty lived in the United States, which automatically added hardship to the idea of a relationship with him. My smile faltered only a little. I did not care. After my cousin's wedding, Rusty pursued me and I pursued him in turn. In spite of seldom seeing each other, we managed to cultivate a blossoming romance with infrequent, long conversations over the phone. I often set an alarm to rise and study at four in the morning, only to find myself writing love letters. For the hope in the future and in the life that Rusty gave me during those difficult formative years at the university, and for the wonderful father that he is, I will be forever grateful. The possibility of a future with Rusty sustained and fueled me during those difficult years. My life consisted of studying, hiking, and daydreaming about the next time I would be seeing him. The weekends were especially hard. On Friday afternoon or Saturday morning, I would drive my grandmother to one of my aunt's houses, forty-five minutes away. My brother would be over at his friend's house, and the maid had the weekend off. I was alone. I would do a morning hike and a late afternoon hike and study in between and for the remainder of the day. For all practical purposes, I was completely alone for the entire weekend.

Those were very long days, days spent in complete silence. I had become master of the art of delayed gratification, a skill that fosters and hones resilience. Sometimes I wouldn't talk to another person until Sunday night, when I drove the forty-five minutes to my aunt's to bring my grandmother back. By the time we got home, Nivea, the maid had arrived too. At last, I had someone to talk with. I missed her. I missed the smell of the cigarettes that she smoked, her lightness and joviality. She had a loud laugh, which oddly enough, had a calming effect on me. She introduced me to one of the most important tools for survival in life: the art of sarcasm, the art of humor, of being able to laugh at myself. She had the ability to find humor in every situation. I was always very serious. I did not know how to laugh. I was used to filtering all my emotions, showing only what I thought was the appropriate thing to show. She taught me how to laugh at myself. She taught me a most important premise: "Nothing is the end of the world." Wisdom comes from unexpected sources.

For Rusty, I made our long-distance relationship my project, and I gave it my all. Our marriage took place in Caracas, coinciding with the end of medical school. I was twenty-four years old. Regretfully, it takes more than will power and intellectual effort and energy to find a soul mate. One has to learn to be still and quiet and to listen to one's intuition, to listen to one's heart. Over the eleven years that we shared, Rusty proved to be a kind, respectful, hard-working, honorable man, but it was not enough for our marriage to survive. Our connection did not run deep enough and the thin, rigid thread that held us together, in its lack of elasticity, was irreparably broken by the strain and stress brought on by the expansion of the family, by the birth of our child.

Trying Times

I had two years of medical school left when my grandmother had the first stroke. At the time she was a diabetic with uncontrolled hypertension, and quite obese. The stroke marked the beginning of the end. In the months that followed, she deteriorated at a rapid rate. She had imaginary phone conversations with people who didn't exist. She started living her life in an imaginary realm. People she didn't know interacted with people who were long dead. It all came together well, at least in her head. She had completely lost touch with reality. It became impossible to hold a simple conversation with her. During this period, I became engaged to Rusty and wanted to share the good news with her. She seemed confused, telling me to be careful since the American soldier that I was about to marry would go to war and I would go with him.

My mother temporarily came home from abroad to oversee the planning of my wedding, and to keep an eye on my grandmother's infamous comforter factory. Soon after her arrival, she paid a visit to the family dentist, a gentleman twenty years her senior, and soon after that she began dating him. We didn't understand what she was doing. No one knew if she was having problems in her marriage in Virginia. No one knew the state of her relationship with my stepfather. I thought it bizarre that she never mentioned him, or that whenever he called the apartment she would disappear into the bathroom or go out to the balcony, closing the sliding door behind her so no one could overhear the conversation.

I did not dwell too much on the awkwardness of this situation, as I had a lot on my plate. I was contemplating doing a medical

residency in the United States, since there were no job opportunities in Venezuela for my future husband. I was planning my
wedding, too. I was researching and learning about the different
anesthesiology residency programs and what the requirements
were for a foreign medical graduate. There were applications to
fill out and exams to sit for. Mainly, the two exams in question
were in the basic science category and in the general clinical
category. Based on the results of those two exams a residency
program would choose you or not. My grandmother (and my
uncle) had given me money to cover the application fees for the
exams. Still, I needed money to buy all the books required to
prepare for the exams.

Once more I called my father and asked him to help me buy
the books. He said he couldn't afford to give me anything. At the
time, we both knew I would be graduating from medical school
with honors. I had proven myself as a medical student. I continued to turn to my father because I didn't want him to tell me,
ever: "If you had asked me for medical books, I would have
given you money for them... medical books... that's something,
you know, that's different."

Yet I couldn't understand how this man who drove the latest
model of the fanciest cars, who owned properties and had in-
vestment accounts all over the world, refused to help me at the
time of my direst need. In the end, my future father-in-law lent
me the money. Once again, I received help from an unexpected
source.

In spite of such distractions, I managed to concentrate and
study very hard for the residency entrance exams. With God's
favor, I did very well, attaining very high grades. My dedicated
effort in the last seven years was paying off, as the combination
of graduating with honors from medical school and the grades
in the entrance examinations opened many doors to many residency programs all over the United States. I made the decision

to seek a position at the University of Miami, where my fiancé lived. His parents and his brother resided closed by and I felt confident I could count on their emotional support.

At the end of my interview with the dean of the anesthesiology program at the University of Miami, he offered me the position on the spot, relieving me from months of waiting to hear from the National Residency Match Program, a nonprofit organization that guides residency programs in picking their future residents. He asked why I wanted to come to the States for my training. In addition to the obvious reason of my husband living in the country, I told him how much I admired the American people, their honesty, their sense of loyalty to their country and to one another, their accountability and their work ethic. At the end of the interview, the dean recommended a book for me to read.

The book, which I had bought as soon as I left the interview, remains one of my favorites: *Democracy in America*, by Alexis De Tocqueville, a French nobleman travelling in America in the early nineteenth century. De Tocqueville was a champion of liberty, democracy and meritocracy, values that sharply contrasted with the European aristocratic regime.

These values also contrasted with the corrupt Chavez regime, where individuals were appointed to positions for which they had no qualifications. To this day, De Tocqueville's observations and predictions remain relevant and accurate.

***

While I was learning about nineteenth century politics, my mother was concocting a new scheme. She told everyone she was permanently staying in Venezuela to plan my wedding and take care of her ill mother. In reality, she did not want to return to the United States because she did not want to work anymore. To financially survive in Caracas, she planned to marry the old family dentist. When she moved in with him, we were shocked. She was still married to our stepfather in the United States, which made her guilty of bigamy.

Right around the time when my mother decided to leave her second husband in the United States and go back to Venezuela, my grandmother reached the apex of generosity with the proteges at the factory. My mother's arrival at the apartment rekindled the hatred between her and my grandmother that my brother and I were so familiar with. The constant fighting resumed, the yelling, the off-color insults. My mother, of course, inserted herself into my grandmother's affairs, taking an interest in the payroll at the comforter factory. She looked at the money going into my grandmother's account at the bank – interest payouts from my grandfather's investments and moneys coming in from buildings and other real estate that he owned – and the funds going out to pay rent for the factory – where the employees actually lived – the raw material to make the comforters, and the labor. Nothing, she quickly concluded, added up. My mother also realized there was no record of any comforter ever being sold, with the exception of the two that my uncle had bought.

"Mama, nothing makes sense here," she said. "Someone is taking your money and you are not even aware of it happening. Look at how much money is being drained from your account! How often do you pay these people?"

My grandmother replied in that manner reserved for her own daughter. "Shut up you idiot! What I do with my money is none of your business and you are just an angry, jealous woman!"

"I am going to take a drive and find out for myself what is really going on there," said my mother, who may be crazy but certainly does not lack in cunning.

One afternoon, early, my mother drove the short distance between my grandmother's apartment and the factory. The first thing that caught her attention was that there was no work being done in the middle of the afternoon. In fact, the main employee, Orfidia, had four giant suitcases on the floor in the middle of the living room, obviously packing for what seemed to be a protracted trip to a land that required winter clothing. At that moment, the inescapable conclusions were: 1) No work was being done at the factory while the wages continued to be collected 2) Orfidia could not afford to travel to any place that had a winter on her wages 3) There was one too many suitcases being packed as Orfidia only had two daughters.

Orfidia and her daughters were shamefaced and shy upon the sudden appearance of my mother. They were trembling when my mother sat down in the living room and asked whose suitcases those were.

"How many people live and work here?" she asked the fat employee.

"Myself and my two daughters, Senora."

My mother continued, "Then why, please tell me, are you packing four suitcases?"

"Senora, I am sorry, we are going away for a month and we need four suitcases" Upstairs a door slammed.

"Who else is here?" my mother demanded. "Who is upstairs?" The entire house fell silent.

"No one," said Orfidia in the smallest possible voice. If she hoped to avoid my mother's probing, Orfidia was to be disappointed.

Leaping to her feet, my mother took the stairs at a gallop, and with each upward step, her anger escalated. She searched every room, opened every door, pulled back every shower curtain. In the last room, she opened the door to a double closet that stood in the middle. There, hiding in the darkness, stood a woman in a nun's habit, with her eyes closed, holding a rosary in her hands, praying.

It was Orfidia's sister, the owner of the fourth suitcase. My mother pulled her into the light. "How dare you! A thief! And you a nun! You are a disgrace! Using your vows to live off of a benevolent widow!" My mother escorted the nun out of the room, out of the factory and onto the street and shut the door behind her. Once again there was silence. Orfidia started whimpering. She knew it was her turn. My mother looked at her in the eye. "As for you, I am giving you 24 hours to gather your things and leave these premises or I'm calling the police. Enough is enough!" The following morning, the terrified women left the factory and were never heard from again. The factory was officially closed. Gratefully, my grandmother was too demented by then to even care.

***

My mother, the bigamist…What followed was a never-ending string of phone calls from my stepfather in Virginia looking for my mother, for his wife. Everyone at the apartment received instructions to never tell him the truth. Instead, we were to cover up for her with the most outrageous lies and explanations we could think up: that she was at my aunts', visiting; that she was at the hairdresser's; that she had gone to lunch with a friend. It hurt me so very much to lie to my stepfather, but I felt I could not break her trust. I did not want to be submerged into the horror of the situation.

Not that her new marriage was working out that well, either. Her new husband refused to give her free rein with his money, as she had expected, and ran the household with a tight fist, particularly when it came to everyday expenses. He was organizing a trip to Europe for the both of them where she had to pay her own way, including the plane ticket and half of the hotel bill, while providing him with the equivalent of a private tour from a European insider (herself) for free. I survived those difficult months before my wedding by focusing on being grateful for the wonderful opportunity that awaited me in the residency program of my choice, in the United States.

Needless to say, the European tour never came to fruition. On another occasion, my mother slipped and fell at his apartment, twisting her ankle. He drove her to the nearest hospital where he happened to have many physician friends, had my mother seen by one of them, an orthopedic specialist. The friend diagnosed and treated my mother practically for free, having charged only for the material to treat my mother's ankle sprain. Back at their apartment, the dentist presented my mother with a bill for the x-rays of her ankle from the radiology department at the hospital. Once again, it fell to my uncle to pay the bill.

My mother had met her match. What a miser the old dentist was turning out to be. Who knew what kind of lies they had told each other. There was much discord between them, as my brother could attest to. Every time they got into a fight, my mother called my brother to involve him in the row of the day, as became more likely, of the night, as she had resumed her habit of sleeping all day and staying up all night. These calls were a form of abuse. For starters, my brother, who was also in medical school, needed his rest at night, or at the very least, his time for studying. Sometimes she merely dialed my brother's number and let the receiver act as a microphone for a shouting match with the dentist. Other times, my mother accused the dentist of hitting her, or she threatened to kill him.

As if my mother's calls were not enough, the dentist called my brother, too. Once he called to advise that my mother had left the apartment with a knife in her hand, totally naked. My brother had to jump in his car and drive up and down the street looking for a naked middle-aged woman carrying a kitchen knife. She did all this, of course, to call attention upon herself, to act out in the worst, most possibly disturbing manner.

For reasons I still don't understand, they never called me in the middle of the night to referee their fights. I was never brought into it. She had saved it all up for her favorite child, her son. He was paying the price for having received something from her earlier on, some crumbs of affection or attention that had hinted of motherly love. Now, he felt powerless to reject her, partly in obedience to the command to "honor thy father and mother," and partly as a generic gentlemanly urge to protect a destitute woman, a woman who now roamed the streets, naked, lost, aimless and armed, the same woman who had carried him in her womb and nurtured him incarnate. He always managed to find her and take her back to her old husband. Until the night when the phone never rang because it had been accidentally left off the hook.

On this occasion, she was not naked. As a matter of fact she was wearing a long, black dress with a matching purse, where she concealed the kitchen knife. No one knew if she walked all night to her final destination, the group of houses where my great-aunts, her mother's sisters, lived with their families (which had been a forty five minute drive) or if she had persuaded an unfortunate taxi driver to take her there in the middle of the night. By whatever means, she had gotten there. She made sure my aunts and all the members of the family witnessed her rage, as she shouted insults and profanities, and scratched all of their cars with the kitchen knife. It was as if she was possessed by the devil himself. She was a veritable Lucifer, the brightest, most beautiful archangel, bringing on her darkness, fighting the light of her elevated intelligence, her delicate beauty, and the unconditional love of her father and her mother.

That incident understandably created bad blood among the members of the family. Many relationships were severed, which in my family meant avoiding the person at all costs, not answering any phone calls or messages from the person in question, and so forth. It was not unusual for those feuds to go on for ten or twenty years. There was never any effort on either part to put themselves in the other person's shoes and to try to forgive each other for the sake of harmony, for the unity of the family.

Life went on. My sister lived in Washington D.C. with her husband, where he sought sobriety, at her urging, at Alcoholic Anonymous meetings. She had not known until too late that he was a hardened drunk. Sometimes those things are imperceptible in a two-week courtship, particularly for someone as naïve and as trusting as my sister. She was having a difficult time. She had no friends and relied on my stepfather for emotional support. Once again, my mother had abandoned her by having returned to Venezuela. My brother was doing well in medical school in spite of my mother's constant outrage.

My brother and I both knew how to do well at school, because it was the only thing we had known, our only source of satisfaction, throughout childhood up to the present. There had been nothing else for us. What a perfect lesson in resilience and delayed gratification those days gave us. To me, medical school gave the gift of friendship, enabling me to befriend people of the highest caliber. For example, my friend Maite, born in Caracas to Spanish parents, and my friend Kirsten, also born in Caracas to German parents. The devastation caused by World War II had brought the parents of these two angels to my world, and for their loyalty, kindness, empathy, wit and intellect I will be forever grateful. My brother had made some good friends in medical school, too.

At least we had that going for us, good, loyal friends that we could count on, and the promise of a worthwhile career. My sister had neither. What she did have was a one-sided relationship with our father. She had always adored him. Other than having paid for her unfinished attempts at college, he had abandoned her almost as thoroughly as he had my brother and me. My father did not know, ever, whether we were in good health or not, if we had any friends or not, what kind of grades we were getting, or what kind of people we socialized with, whether, at any point in our lives, we had enough to eat and sufficient clothes to wear. Neither he nor my mother was ever able to master the basic pillars of parenthood, the basic tenets of bringing up another human being, a child.

Perhaps my sister had experienced a glimpse of unconditional love on his behalf, during the six years that she had been an only child, although I don't think it very probable. Perhaps she, like my brother, had savored and treasured whatever crumbs had been thrown at her, rendering her into a state of permanent hunger and neediness. As for myself, even though my mother had rejected me when I was born because I had been "another girl" and she had wanted a boy, I knew that while in the womb, she had prayed for me, for my well-being, that during those nine months she had wanted me and she had been excited about me. During the months spent in her womb, I had received unconditional love. And that little bit of unconditional love, passed on to me from the moment of conception until my birth, in spite of having been finite, had been enough to sustain me, to carry me through in life, attesting to the immense power of a mother's unconditional love, even if experienced only for a few months, while in the womb.

***

My grandmother grew sicker and sicker. We suspected the end was near. Every morning, at breakfast, she complained of being very tired from not being able to fall asleep. When asked why she wouldn't rest during the night, she explained that my grandfather (who had been long dead by then) was at the foot at the bed and kept talking and gesturing to her all night. She insisted on telling us how she begged him to leave her alone and let her sleep and he would keep going at it, all night long. That's when we knew. My uncle told me that one week before the massive stroke that had killed my grandfather, he had told both my uncle and my mother that he had been having the strangest dreams, dreams about his eldest brother, Alfredo, who had already passed, and about Alfredo's friends, who had also passed; and that he had not thought about his brother or the friends in forty years. The dreams kept repeating themselves until the night of the stroke.

I often think about how comforting it is to know that my grandfather was waiting for my grandmother at the moment of her passing, in the same way his eldest brother must have been waiting for him when his time had come. I cannot think of a more reassuring feeling than having the certainty that the energy of our loved, lost ones lives forever and will come to meet us and guide us at the time of our crossing over. My heart is bursting with joy, with hope, knowing that someone will be waiting for me when my time comes, that love lives forever and that spirit never dies. Two weeks after my grandfather's ghostly visits to my grandmother had begun, she suffered a stroke of such magnitude that it completely interrupted all functions of higher mental processes. She was in the Intensive Care Unit for a few days, the doctors waiting for any kind of improvement. She remained unresponsive and was moved out of the unit to a private room, where she fell into a coma. Her agonal breathing sustained her for the time that had been needed for all of her relatives and friends to come and tell her goodbye.

I was standing next to her, very close to her bed, when all of a sudden, her eyes, which had been closed since the stroke, opened. She looked to a corner, and then up, and at that very moment she had smiled at whatever she was seeing, and then she smiled at all of us, her face recovering, for what seemed like a few seconds, the youth and the life of earlier years, for all of us to see. That had been her goodbye.

Thank you, grandmother. Thank you, for all that you were and all that you did, for me and for so many others, during so many years. Grandmother, I love you, rest in peace. At the funeral, I helped carry the coffin. How could I not, when she had carried me all my life?

***

The day of my graduation from medical school finally arrived. Fortunately, there had only been one incident of strike at the University. A strike meant the complete suspension of classes and lectures, usually as a mean of protest on behalf of the professors. This particular strike lasted only five months; during which I had been hired by a foreign language academy to teach English. The teaching had kept me occupied for a few hours every day, though not enough to appease my anxiety and unrest. Waiting for the strike to come to a halt and for classes to resume was nerve racking. Every day that went by and the professors at the university had not reached an agreement with the administrative body felt like an eternity of wasted time. It proved also to be the perfect exercise in patience, and in trusting life.

It turned out I needed my wisdom teeth taken out, followed by a protracted recovery, the tissues in my mouth becoming infected and inflamed. The infection had taken a hold of the friable tissues in spite of having had two complete weeks of apparently uneventful healing; that is, until the morning when I had awoken to very swollen and tender cheeks and gums, generalized malaise and a temperature of one hundred and two. I went back to the dentist who had performed the operation, who diagnosed an abscess in my gum. After a thorough cleaning of the affected area, I went home with a sore mouth, a headache and a prescription for a two-week course of antibiotics.

Back at the apartment, the maid had lovingly prepared freshly squeezed pineapple juice, to decrease the inflammation. I gulped a big glass of the pineapple juice and went straight to my room, to sleep. After an hour's nap, I stayed in bed, resting, and picked up my copy of Rilke's *Letters to a Young Poet*. I opened it to a page, randomly, without much thought. A particular phrase caught my eye: "Let life happen to you. Believe me: life is in the right, always." I closed the book, closed my eyes, and savored the moment. I felt grateful, grateful because the professors at the university were on strike and I would be able to rest and take all the time I needed to heal, without having to worry about falling behind in class. Grateful for life's perfect timing.

As the years have gone by, over and over, I have realized this: Everything happens for a reason, that in life there are no coincidences, only lessons, and that life is always working with us, for us, lending itself as the perfect classroom in which we will learn the lessons that are due to be learned and that will make us grow, emotionally and spiritually. My gums made a perfect recovery and I had even made a little money at the language academy when the professors and the university reached an agreement and the doors to the portal of knowledge reopened, at last.

Lonely At The Top

Preparations were well underway for graduation, which was to take place at the Aula Magna, the big auditorium at the main campus of the university. I invited both my father and my mother. I was quite curious to see if my father would come, in the first place, and also, if my mother would come, knowing that my father had been invited too. I was excited, proud of my achievement, having graduated with honors, with a Magna Cum Laude distinction. The morning of the ceremony, the Aula Magna was brimming with the good cheer of family and friends who had gathered to celebrate with the graduates. My father did come, with his third wife and children. I was so very happy.

The graduating students sat in the front. When my turn came to walk up to the podium and receive my diploma, as the master of ceremonies announced my name and my academic distinction, I turned around and looked back. The entire auditorium stood up for me, in recognition to my effort, to my journey. I accepted the golden medals that the Rector of the university placed around my neck with tears of joy. In addition to graduate honors, they presented me two additional awards, one for Academic Excellence, the other in recognition of my outstanding academic record in the subjects of physiology and pharmacology. The second award was perfectly suited for my chosen specialty, anesthesiology.

After the ceremony, we went outside to meet our families and take graduation pictures. I saw my mother. We hugged. Then, the frantic search for my father began. He was nowhere to be found. I walked and walked and looked and looked, in vain. I called his phone. He answered normally, with no particular tone of embarrassment or concern. I asked him where he was, telling him I wanted to take a picture with him. Coldly, he explained that he was no longer there, that he had left in the middle of the graduation because it was taking too long and he had been bored and tired. I couldn't bring myself to say anything to him. I hung up the phone and went back to take pictures with the ones who were there, my mother and my brother.

My father had promised me a graduation ring. I visited the jewelry store several times to pick it up because every time I had called to ask him about it, he assured me that the ring had been ready. I went to the jewelry store three times. Three times I was told that the ring had not been paid for. My father had lied or what was worse, he had it all planned so that it would be me or someone else who would end up paying for the ring. My mother, in an effort to console me, told me that the medals from the graduation, with my name engraved on the back, were much more meaningful than whatever ring he was refusing to pay for. For once her words rang true to my ears.

***

On the other hand, the preparations for my wedding unlocked the latest craze in my mother. For her, a relative lack of money for the whole endeavor was the main stressor. At the time, it was customary, among my mother's class in Venezuela, to have a reputable fashion house individually design a wedding gown for the bride. That was simply not an option for me. My uncle telephoned my father, requesting his financial involvement in the wedding. My father's answer had been that he was in a financial bind and that there was not even the slightest possibility that he could contribute anything. My uncle, in his generosity and compassion, offered to give me five thousand dollars for my wedding. It was that gift which allowed me to have a nice reception at the ballroom of one of the local hotels.

Still, the three months preceding the wedding were a relentless effort to get some money, any money, out of my father to cover some of the expenses. I literally went to his house and begged. He lived in a high rise with his new family, together with a cook, a maid and a chauffeur who doubled as a butler and was made to wear white gloves while on duty. I hated going there so I devised a plan to make the visits and the begging more palatable. I brought people with me, whoever was available. My brother's girlfriend came along, several friends both from high school and medical school. Their job was to entertain my father's wife so I would get a chance to talk to my father alone, and hopefully, soften his heart. The plan eventually worked. At the end of the visits, my father agreed to pick up the bill for the limousine that would drive my fiancé and myself from the church to the reception, and for the orchestra that would be providing the entertainment. I thanked him profusely for both.

The following issues remained to be solved: the wedding dress, the wedding cake, and finding a professional or at least semi-professional singer for the ceremony, to sing the "Ave Maria" at church. I was anxious about the wedding cake and the singer. One of my grandmother's sisters had offered a wedding cake and a lady to sing in the church during the ceremony. My mother had rejected the gesture. It was a matter of pride for her, being in the middle of a big feud with all of my grandmother's sisters at the time. Five days before the wedding, coming to the realization that we had no money for either the singer or the cake, my mother changed her mind.

In her usual manner of doing things, she knocked hysterically on my door at a quarter to four in the morning. "Open up! You idiot, open up! Get up and call your aunt and let her know you want the cake and the singer! Right now." I was terrified. She had the same tone of voice as when I was eleven and she had kicked me out of the house in the middle of the winter, the same night when she tried to kill herself "because of me." I rose from bed and opened the door, my heart in my throat, fearing that she was going to throw herself at me, hitting and slapping me. I had no memory of having done anything to anger her so much in the past few days.

My aunt answered the phone. Embarrassed, crying on the phone, I explained to her that I was calling at four o'clock in the morning because my mother had wanted me to, and that she was standing there next to me, and that I was terrified. I told her to please arrange for the cake and the singer and I thanked her for everything. My mother left the room in silence and closed the door behind her. I never went back to sleep. That was the beginning of my pre-nuptial insomnia. For almost the entire week right before the wedding, I was unable to fall asleep, and the few times I did fall asleep it lasted for twenty minutes, an hour maximum. I was anxious and scared, and felt completely surrounded by the biggest dread. In the embarrassment of my shame, I hid all my emotions from my future husband, robbing him of the opportunity to grow closer to me and to offer some emotional support.

***

The morning of my wedding, I felt and looked exhausted, haggard and drawn. The truth was that I was relieved. After that day there would be nothing else to fear, no more fretting over the dress or the cake, no more fearing about what my mother would do or say at the wedding. My mother found an acceptable wedding dress, very cheap, in the not-so-good part of town. I will never forget the look in my mother's eyes, as the make-up artist had finished her job and I put on the dress.

She looked at me, her eyes running up and down, over my face, on the dress and back on my face. It was a look of disdain and disgust. I wanted to cry, feeling ashamed and rejected by the icon of beauty, elegance and class that my mother was considered to be by everyone. Memories of the question she had asked me when I had gotten engaged raced through my mind: "Are you sure he wants to marry you? Don't you think that since you met him at your cousin's wedding and your cousin's reception took place at her godmother's mansion, that he wants to marry you because he thinks you may be rich, too? You really haven't given that possibility a thought?"

At that moment I just wanted my wedding to be over. This hurt too much. I wanted everyone gone, the celebrations cancelled. Living hurt. It hurt and I didn't feel like hurting anymore. I walked out of the room in which I was getting dressed, looking down, in despair. My brother and his angel girlfriend came up to me.

"Don't pay any attention to her," my brother said. "She is going around like a crazy lady talking about our father and her divorce."

I managed to collect myself. I managed a smile, unable to foresee my mother's last charade, her "Last Supper." Rusty, walked into the church with his mother by his side. His mother, a beautiful Englishwoman, had chosen a turquoise blue gown to match her eyes. She was a picture of elegance. My uncle, the only real fatherly figure, gave me away that night.

"I am entrusting her to you, honor her and love her," he had told Rusty at the altar. I teared upon hearing his words.

No one was prepared for what came next. I, the bride, had already entered the church, the entire wedding party having taken their seats, when all of a sudden, at the last minute, my mother paraded down the central aisle, with her husband, the old dentist. I was looking at the giant crucifix behind the altar when the commotion made me turn around: there she was, smiling, coming down the aisle, in all her glory, wearing a black dress. She had to enter the church last, after the bride, in black.

She had to have the last word, as usual, because in the end, it was all about her, and it would always be all about her.

In the end, very few people attended the wedding. The majority of my friends were away for the summer. The singer at the church was pitiful. The reception was nice. Preoccupied and on edge, I was out of touch with my new husband and I did not want my brother to leave. I stayed next to him until the morning, dreading the final moment of separation: my departure for the United States...Another devastating red flag about the unsuitability of Rusty and I as a couple that was altogether missed.

***

I settled down quickly and seamlessly in my adopted country. I felt at home right away, embracing all the new acquaintances, making new friends, capitalizing on my ability to adapt to new environments and people. I missed nothing about Venezuela. I returned only once in that period, to attend my brother's own wedding. Being in a foreign country was a fresh opportunity to thrive, to be emotionally free, in the same way my stay at the English boarding school had given me a fresh, positive outlook on life.

This emotional bonanza, this feeling of novelty and opportunity and of healthy disconnection from the horrors of The Big House and the apartment did not last long. My mother wanted to visit her two daughters in the United States. The first stop would be my house. She arrived with several suitcases, which seemed a little bit suspicious. She stayed for a few days with me. To my relief, it was a peaceful, uneventful visit. I would never have imagined what she did afterwards.

The truth was that she had purchased a one-way ticket. She wasn't planning on returning to the family dentist. She left the old man, unexpectedly, without saying a word, to rejoin her second husband, my stepfather. They would stay together until the time of his death. Once my mother arrived in Virginia and moved back in with my stepfather, she went out of control. Again. My brother had made the mistake of allowing my father to be in his wedding. My mother never forgave him for that. My brother was visiting my mother and stepfather for the weekend, alone, without his wife, during the internship year of his cardiology residence. He had decided to take a shower in the middle of the day. My mother took a wire hanger, untwisted it out of shape, and used one of the ends of the wire to open the bathroom door that my brother had locked.

My brother was not even been aware of her presence in the bathroom when she pulled back the shower curtain, and with a sharp knife, slashed open the vein in her left forearm, as she calmly said: "This is to remind you that you were born in this blood and not in your father's blood."

My brother jumped from the shower to hold pressure on the wound, tying his shirt around her bleeding arm. He came out of the bathroom dragging her behind him, screaming, urging my stepfather to call an ambulance. My brother said that the worst part had been having to spend the night with her at the hospital, sitting on a chair next to her bed, sleepless, as she slept a deep chemically induced sleep, and, following the doctor's orders, telling her he loved her when she woke up.

After a several days at the psychiatric ward, my mother was finally diagnosed. So far, both in Venezuela and in Europe, she had been given the diagnosis of major depression and anxiety. She had been on heavy tranquilizers and antidepressants beginning in her adolescence. The doctors at the hospital called us with the news. The former diagnoses she had carried all her life were correct, but that had not been all. In addition, my mother had borderline personality disorder and psychosis. A person with borderline personality disorder is extremely sensitive to environmental circumstance. The perception of impending separation or rejection leads to profound changes in self-image, cognition and behavior. They exhibit a pattern of unstable and intense interpersonal relationships, alternating between extremes of idealization and devaluation, emotional instability, recurrent suicidal behavior and inappropriate, intense anger.

She was placed on large doses of antipsychotics and made to go to therapy for life. At first, my brother and I panicked, not knowing if we could also develop the latter portion of the diagnosis. We cried together, over the phone, realizing that in spite of knowing all the components of her mental illness, the pain accumulated over the past twenty-five years had not eased and would probably never would. I did feel some pity and compassion for her, and for my grandparents and my uncle for what they had been through.

I knew, however, that her three children had been affected the most, our sense of self being profoundly damaged by her disease. We would always live on the outside, observing ourselves through the eyes of others, our sense of self-worth dependent upon other people's reactions to us, and on other people's reactions to our achievements and our perceived flaws.

I couldn't remember a time when my core emotions had not been sadness and emptiness, my childhood environment having been one of constant, sharp criticism and disabling cruelty. The more I read about my mother's diagnosis, the more I identified the traits of a damaged child of a borderline parent in myself. I realized I walked around terrified of others, feeling tremendous fear and overwhelming anxiety about what they thought of me. I assumed people were angry with me much of the time, and why not? My mother was. I felt responsible for other people's moods and sadness and tried to fix them at all costs. I was disproportionately giving in my relationships, in money and time, in doing favors for people and fixing their lives.

I was high highly critical of myself and others, I had a black-and-white mentality when it came to viewing them as well. They were either demons or saints, in my mind existed no middle ground. I had an irrational fear of abandonment and rejection. The most disabling part, however, was the inability to realize that emotions were not thoughts, that the emotions I felt did not reflect reality. The emotions that I so intensely felt created a narrative of twisted thinking that perpetuated my sadness and emptiness. It was a vicious cycle my circumstances had created but that I'd have to combat.

The most difficult part was the awareness of the enormous emotional damage my mother had inflicted on me and would continue to impact me as long as I allowed her in my life. How does one severe ties completely with one's mother? How does one undo the damage? With every passing year, I have gained insight on the far-reaching implications of being the daughter of a borderline mother. Constant self-examination and awareness of wrong, distorted thinking have been pivotal in the journey. Keeping her at a distance and setting physical and emotional boundaries have afforded me some protection. I never managed to disconnect myself completely from her. She is my mother, after all, you know. Blood of her blood.

And my father?... During my medical residency he called once, unexpectedly. Initially he said he needed my help with something very important. "I'm going up to Miami to do some shopping," he announced. "Research the area looking for black leather jackets." Apparently, it was of utmost importance that he buy an expensive leather jacket. For himself. "Okay," I told him, bemused. "I will do my best."

"I also have a big surprise for you," he said. "But I want to deliver it in person."

Naturally, I assumed the surprise was to be a present for me. Despite a lifetime of parsimony, neglect, and selfishness when it came to his children, I started daydreaming. Maybe, just maybe, he repented of his miserliness and actually had something for me: plans for a trip together, a birthday present, as my birthday was right around the corner. Maybe he even wanted to begin repairing our warped and damaged relationship.

After he flew into Miami, we met at Fat Tuesdays in The Grove for lunch. He had with him his blond paramour, now his wife, and her child, Wilmer, plus a little girl about six years of age. This was my youngest half-sister, the last of my father's seven offspring, by three different women. The girl was a quiet, delicate child. My husband, Rusty, watched attentively as my father interacted with his youngest daughter. My father was playing with her, caressing her, laughing with her. I watched too, desperately trying to pretend that I was watching a pair of strangers, a loving father and his little girl, playing together. I tried to pretend he had no relation to me, trying not to think too much about it, looking around, sipping my Diet Coke.

Then, my husband asked, referring to me: "What was she like when she was six years old?"

My father answered without hesitation: "Her? I wouldn't know. The way I am with these two, I was never with her."

I wanted to get up and go home. I did my best to block the tears. Whatever scar tissue had been forming around the wound, my father had destroyed with one thoughtless remark. This, however, was but the beginning. Next my father revealed his big surprise for me. "I have lost forty pounds!" he declared, slapping his abdomen. I sat there motionless, wide-eyed, as though the boastful smack to his belly had been a thunderclap, right next to me. For a moment I was dazed, unable to hear, or process what was going on around me.

As my senses returned, a realization came with them—a realization I might have made long before if I had not had the hope of an unloved child for a parental change of heart. I realized at last that his selfishness was pathological, a kind of emotional or cognitive birth defect. He was unable to process certain things and unable to feel certain others. Whatever he had experienced in his life had done nothing to make him grow up. My father was the most immature, selfish man I would ever interact with. In the days following this meeting, I came to acknowledge that I would have to be grateful he had not passed on this disability to me. Otherwise the pain of growing up as his daughter, and my equally maladjusted mother, might curdle into a bitterness that could blight the rest of my life, too.

**

My internal medicine internship at Jackson Memorial Hospital was a trying time for a foreign medical graduate. Most of the medical terms, medical conditions, diagnostic tools and tests I only knew in the Spanish language. To eventually master all the medical jargon was almost like learning a new language. Learning the correct pronunciation of the new vocabulary was also trying—in the English language, the same letter can be pronounced in many ways. There are no general rules to memorize when it comes to pronunciation, no choice but to individually memorize the correct pronunciation for each word.

Once the initial shock of the terminology passed, and I became more acclimated to working in English, I encountered a second level of difficulty which consisted in memorizing the acronyms that are commonly used in this country. For example, ESRD means renal failure (End Stage Renal Disease); CAD is Coronary Artery Disease. I found no short cuts. Each acronym had to be learned in its turn.

Despite the immersion in the daily grind of the forming years, I still managed to cherish and collect precious moments of human interaction which were fun. Friendships are fun—especially when you play matchmaker with your friends! I introduced a fellow intern, Ruby, who would eventually become a hematologist-oncologist, to our neighbor and good friend, Keith. In spite of their different background (she was Filipino and he was a Jewish New Yorker) theirs was a perfect match, very nearly love at first sight. It was also as if I lived whatever romance and passion my marriage lacked through the romantic relationships of others. Still, I made the mistake so many women in lukewarm relationships make: thinking that having a baby will enhance their dull lives and "fix" whatever is lacking or missing in the relationship. In addition, I was thirty two years old and my maternal instinct was no longer dormant: I was determined to become a mother.

A Mother's Love Is Always In Its Spring

Did I always want to be a mother? A rabbit hole is dark, long and deep, heavy with the weight of expectation; terrifying, as one falls down it, blindly, holding fast to one's child in order to not lose him, to not make mistakes, to not be condemned. A maze is equally terrifying: the overwhelming task of not losing one's child in it; the life mission of finding our way amidst the walls that have wide open eyes and ears, and crossings that have sharp tongues to criticize and wound, sometimes fatally. One is always afraid and one never feels ready enough.

Still, in my adolescent bedroom, in my virgin bed, I found myself wide awake at two am in the morning, twice. The light green sheets drenched in sweat, my body frozen in the cold wet-ness, wide awake from the nightmare, barely able to move, my tongue stuck inside my mouth and my lips dry as a bone. A faint ray of streetlight entered through the only gap between the curtain and the gray wall opposite my bed, not bright or wide enough to rule out unwanted presences or distorted objects that, in my hyperalert mind, set out to be non gratae beings in the stillness and darkness of the night. In those nightmares, I had found out that I was pregnant.

Pregnant at twenty-one. Pregnant with fear and disgust for myself, for my so far unworthy life because I had attained nothing yet and therefore had nothing to show for it. Pregnant with failure, with the sacrifice of my own life cut short, my plans for the future automatically discarded and eliminated so that someone else who, God knows why, had chosen my womb to incarnate, could get a go at life, a go at this never-ending merry go round that stops for no one, ever. The abomination of the idea of being pregnant had the strongest, impenetrable hold in my psyche. Twelve long years would have to go by before the tentacles of paralyzing fear, wrapped tightly around my entire being, would start to loosen up, to become slightly porous, to begin to weaken and to let in some light, allowing the cautious and most careful exploration of a sliver of the future, an imagined, optional future, perhaps just an image, an idea. A possibility of me being able to be a good mother, an image of me with a child in my arms, or next to me, who smiled and was happy because I knew how to make him happy. The image of a child who smiled because his mother or her mother was a good mother and knew how to make him or her happy felt unattainable, highly improbable if not impossible. In my mind, the absence of any childrearing templates in my life made it so.

The friends and acquaintances from high school started going steady with their boyfriends, who would eventually and inevitably become their fiancés in a society where most marriages and relationships are crafted, supported and maintained by the groom and bride's respective families. The wedding receptions were magnificent to say the very least. A modest, low profile reception had the attendance of a minimum of five hundred guests, and two different orchestras provided the entertainment throughout the evening. The flutes and tumblers of the guests, young and old, were continuously filled to the brim with champagne, whisky, or rum of the highest quality, while the most exquisite hors d'oeuvres were offered by a veritable army of professional waitstaff. An elegant sit-down dinner heralded undoubtedly by a velouté cream soup, which was always perfect, followed by two or three courses of delicately prepared entrees, awaited the guests.

Who, ever, had room for dessert? Everybody did! The wedding cake was an immaculate, out of this world creation. Who, in their sane minds, would dare forego a piece of heaven on earth? And the dancing continued until the late hours of the night or the very early hours of the morning, until the liquor would run out or the sun would rise. Then, it was time to go for breakfast at one of the twenty four hour service "Areperas" or corn cakes restaurants, interspersed among the fast food selling places in the capital, where by now, the very drunk and certainly very amused guests looked for one last morsel of sustenance, one last moment of entertainment. And, then, a couple of years later, the triumphant announcement of the pregnancy, which, in short, was a yearlong pass for unproductive inactivity, for doing absolutely nothing.

I, certainly, took part in the congratulatory ritual and ceremony of their Baby Showers, not without the slightest feeling of schadenfreude (and relief) that it was them and never, God forbid, me. Then, the mandatory nine months of doing nothing but fatten up and be ready for the delivery of the baby.

In my particular case, being a housewife was the fastest, quickest way to boredom and unhappiness, with no personal goals to attain and absolutely no personal challenges to overcome. My own mother a shining example of this phenomenon. A career would come first, a challenging career, I promised myself. I held on to that promise until I felt an important milestone had been reached, the solidity and stability of a good job, a safe opportunity at a long standing, well established place. That's where my personal ordeal with the inability to get pregnant began. Oh the audacity of God, Oh the impertinence of the Universe, the sarcasm of life...for sure all of them laughing, hysterically, behind my back; at my fear of an unwanted pregnancy, at my relief of not being the one who was pregnant, at those nightmares, those night terrors of long ago. Who would have guessed? Who could have known?

Fortunately, at a place and time in life where many women had no options, I had options. I had affluency and the greatest and priceless gift of all gifts, time. I was blessed with time and money to shop around for the most successful infertility specialist back then. And so, began the arduous journey of trying to get pregnant, in retrospect the most difficult one for someone who was used to putting in the work, getting the desired results and moving on to the next goal. Getting pregnant doesn't work like that. It is unpredictable, unexpected, offering no logical explanations or giving out promises. One cannot make it happen, even if one tries one's hardest, one cannot control any of the variables or the events. The only certainty when one is trying to conceive a baby is the myriad of doctor's appointments, of questionnaires waiting to be filled out, of blood tests and prescriptions and… waiting. Waiting for a result, for a blood test result, for an ovulation test or a pregnancy test or for a phone call to be returned. This was the hardest, crassest course in patience thrown at me by the master teacher: life.

The first specialist correctly diagnosed my Polycystic Ovarian Syndrome, a condition where, as a result of an imperfect hormonal milieu, I was unable to ovulate. Having dealt with irregular periods all my life, I quickly accepted this diagnosis as the sole cause of my infertility. Off I went to fill out a prescription for clomiphene, a drug that hyper stimulated my ovaries and would, fingers crossed, make me ovulate. Prescription in hand, the pharmacist looked up and took his glasses off, taking a step back. "Excuse me, Miss, with all due respect, are you sure they wrote for the correct amount?" I looked at him, in silence, trying to find something to say. "The thing is, Miss, you look tiny to me." At one hundred milligrams a pill for thirty days, it did sound a bit too much for my slight frame and small size, I admitted to myself. I pushed the thought away, in my desperation to conceive.

I did manage a response, although hesitant: "I assure you, sir, there is no mistake in this prescription. When will it be ready?"

The pharmacist looked down, moving his head from left to right and from right to left. One hundred milligrams of clomiphene, every day, at the same time, washed down with the sweet, simple flavor of orange juice, my husband's favourite: a simple recipe for happiness. Only that the ovulation tests kept reassuring me that I was indeed ovulating, but for some strange reason, I was not getting pregnant. The only thing to report after nine years of marriage and the clomiphene experiment was a ten-pound weight gain and no baby!

The morning after the last failed pregnancy test, I was assigned to provide anesthesia at an ambulatory surgical center, which was part of the hospital where I worked. My first case was listed as a Dilation and Curettage, a simple D and C. Little did I know the turning of events that would take place on that Monday morning. I prepared Operating Room number one, where all the gynecological procedures usually took place. Pushing the surgical mask down, away from my face, I entered the preop holding area, where the patients awaiting surgery were getting ready for their procedures. It was a busy room, with some of the nurses filling out forms and charts for the patients, others starting intravenous infusions and taking and recording vital signs. My patient was almost ready, the nurse securing and taping down the catheter in her vein for the fluids. She was very young and scared. Her small face was red from crying and her eyes were closed. She seemed to be either praying or mumbling something to herself.

"Good morning! I am your anesthesiologist. How are you this morning?" She looked away. "I am going to have you answer some questions, please." She would still not face me. I asked the nurse if there was a relative or a friend with her in the waiting room outside.

The nurse pulled me aside. "This is her second abortion and she is only seventeen! She is extremely embarrassed and doesn't want to talk to anyone. We got her to give a medical history after 15 minutes of begging and convincing. She came alone, in a taxi. There are no parents and no known father of the baby. She is sixteen weeks pregnant." I looked back at my patient, terrified, ashamed, lying on the stretcher. How I secretly wished it were me who was pregnant and not her. I quickly reviewed the responses she had given to the nurse and proceeded to wheel her back to OR one, not without reassuring her everything was going to be fine and that I would take good care of her. The sedatives I gave her as part of the induction drug cocktail helped her to relax, at last. She went to sleep trusting, exhausted.

I couldn't hold my tongue as the surgeon walked in, scrubbed, holding his hands up in the air waiting for the surgical technician to gown and glove him. "God feeds those who have no teeth with which to chew their food." I announced, starting a long lament over my infertility. The surgeon quickly interrupted: "Has anyone tested your husband for any issues? At this point, it would be wrong to assume that it is all on you, especially after several rounds of one hundred milligrams of clomiphene on someone your size," he very calmly offered. "Come see me in my office. We can talk. I find it so hard to believe that no one has tested your husband" There it was! My epiphany! My second opinion, laid out in front of me, waiting for me on a Monday morning at a surgical center... Life has its ways. It never fails.

As it turned out to be, there was an issue with the quality of the sperm in question. A small issue that would end up taken care of by the use of a reproductive complex and the avoidance of saunas and hot baths. The only problem, which was not so small by then, was that my system was not responding to the clomiphene after months of hyperstimulation. I stopped ovulating. At that point, my options were to either have surgery to lyse the tissue around the ovaries and improve the hormonal response or continue to hyper stimulate the ovaries with even more potent drugs to induce ovulation. I chose the former. It was the correct choice. Within two months of the surgery I had a positive pregnancy test: Joy to the world!

During my pregnancy, I never knew what being nauseated or edematous was. I never waddled or felt dizzy; nor did I ever fall asleep when and where I was not supposed to. One could say those twelve months of infertility and uncertainty paid forward in the form of a happy, easy, almost delightful pregnancy.

My body responded beautifully to carrying another body inside it. There were other difficulties awaiting, though. My mother, who had been in Virginia for quite some time at this point, decided to visit her soon mother-to-be daughter. My husband Rusty, confident in the positivity and general state of happiness that normally surrounds expecting families, welcomed her with open arms. The night of her arrival, as Rusty got home from work and changed into jeans and a green t-shirt (my favourite colour), Lytton, our straight haired brown dachshund, our first son, gnawed incessantly on his little bed. From time to time he would nervously look up and let out a whimper. All the while Rusty was gone Lytton was restless and appeared uncomfortable. I offered him a beef chew that went completely ignored. I offered him his favourite toy, a squeaky rubber rooster. That did not distract him either.

Two hours went by and I didn't know what to do with him, until the garage door opened and in walked Rusty, loaded with suitcases and bags, in his best rendition of a mule, followed by my mother, who carried a purse, two handbags and a supermarket plastic bag filled with empty potato chip bags and bottles of Diet Coke. Lytton jumped out of his little bed and went straight to Rusty. My mother approached the pair bending down to pet Lytton, who, at that moment, turned into the most ferocious Pitbull that ever existed. I had to pick him up and take his bed and his toys to the master bedroom in order for the barking to subside. Fifteen minutes later, from the master bedroom, I heard the screams.

I don't know who started it. All I know is that I came out of the bedroom to find my mother chasing my husband with a glass of water in her hands. He managed to lock himself up in one of the guest bedrooms, moments before she thrusted the glass of water at said door with every ounce of strength she was able to muster. "Stop, mother, stop!" I cried out, once more, afraid, paralyzed in her presence. She turned around and calmly said "This will not end here; I am calling the police so they take him away for domestic violence" And call the police she did. A loud knock on the door followed.

Two policewomen entered our living room and searched the place as Lytton went around and around the coffee table, in a frenzy. He wouldn't stop. Once again, I had to carry him in my arms.

"Officers, I am so sorry that my mother made you come out here for nothing. My husband is not a violent man and he has never lay a hand on anyone, including my mother." I picked up my mother's purse and took out a plastic, transparent bag which held no less than a dozen bottles of pills. "Officers, she is not well as you can see by the number of pills she takes every few hours." Lytton jumped down from my arms and started to run around in circles, very fast, manically.

"I am sorry but they cannot spend the night in this house together. One of them has to go." I looked around, nervously. I didn't want to be alone with her either, but it was the best option for everyone. Rusty stepped up, announced he was spending the night elsewhere, took Lytton with him and drove to a nearby hotel that, fortunately, accepted pets.

Then came the apologies. "I am so sorry, please forgive me for what I have done to you both and for putting the baby at risk. I am coming back to drive you to the hospital and keep you company and to help with the delivery and the first few months with the baby." It was the litany she repeated over and over because she knew she had "fallen from favor" with the father of the baby.

I was relieved, in a way. I knew that she wouldn't help me or do anything for me. She was incapable of doing such things. She had never done it for any of her three children; having always had baby nurses and nannies and maids at her disposition preventing her from changing a diaper, helping with a feeding or even lifting one manicured finger. I knew she would come to my house to be taken care of and served, like a princess. I realized I would be without her during the delivery of the baby. But at least I knew I would have peace of mind.

The due date approached fast. I considered myself to be well prepared for what was coming and also worked until the very end; the contractions starting in the operating room as I gave my last anesthetic, at thirty-eight weeks of pregnancy. For several hours after I had arrived at the maternity hospital where my son would be born, I was on the phone with friends and with my brother, joking, laughing, and sharing stories. At nine o'clock that night the phone calls stopped. I couldn't talk anymore, doubled over in pain, in pain that was so excruciating all sense of dignity or embarrassment were lost. With every contraction I was certain my insides were being ripped apart.

Rusty didn't know what to do to comfort me; he didn't even know what to do with himself. He sat on the guest chair, motionless, looking out the window, his breathing heavy with unease. In my usual state of defensiveness, I concluded he was either angry or bored. "Feel free to go home if you are tired," I managed between the contractions. I completely misread him and remained convinced, for years to come, that he didn't care about me, that he had no love for me.

"How could anyone love me, if my own parents didn't even want me?" I asked myself, the contractions making everything worse. The delivery room nurse "kept my pain at bay" with a sedative that never took the pain away. It just made me doze off for as long as the contraction subsided. Every forty-five minutes I would sit up in bed like a bolt and cry from the pain.

At four in the morning my cervix was exactly four centimeters dilated. The nurse called anesthesia overhead for an epidural. I positioned myself perfectly on the edge of the bed, arching my back "like an angry cat" and "pushing the needle away from me" like I had many times instructed my patients to do. Relief came, at last. Yet it was painfully short lived. At eight in the morning my water broke. The moment of truth! The baby was coming! The attending obstetrician was called emergently. I pushed, pushed hard, moving the baby, causing his head to be finally crowned by the birth canal. My perfect son, my little boy was out in the world, all six pounds and one ounce of him, crying, cold. I held him on my chest, as he fed for the very first time, in perfect bonding. My long, skinny boy, flesh of my flesh, blood of my blood. Beloved son, I love you and I will always protect you. I will never leave you and I will give my life for you. I pray that I am an adequate mother for you. Please forgive me for all the mistakes I am going to make. I will not know better but I promise you I will always do my best.

Becoming a mother changed me, in many ways. For starters, I could not bring myself to provide anesthesia for women seeking terminations of pregnancy anymore, regardless of their gestational age. I became aware of other babies and children wherever I happened to be. It was as if the well-being of each and every child in the world had become my responsibility. I felt true pain whenever I thought of all the mothers, especially the single ones, and the very young ones, who adored and loved their babies in the same way I loved mine and who couldn't afford to feed and clothe them, let alone spend time with them, many times having to work two jobs just to be able to provide for them.

So strong was this feeling of injustice for the helpless mothers of the world that I committed to providing for a boy, the same age as my son, in Guatemala, through "Children International," a charity organization that provided me with pictures of the child and handwritten letters when the time came. I felt I was making a sliver of a difference, amongst all those children, for the little boy in Guatemala and for his parents, and I toyed with the idea of adopting a child in the future. I cried over the communist orphanages in Romania, Ceausescu's children, babies who rocked themselves to sleep, always alone, and who stopped crying because their cries were no longer heard by anyone, and nobody came. I teared for all those abandoned babies whose parents couldn't take care of them. I felt, especially, for the older ones who nobody wanted and who would never get adopted. Perhaps I could foster an older child, a teenager, and spoil them with my time and attention, with nice clothes and nice things that would make them feel special and at least, momentarily, make them forget about their pain. I would be the person I needed when I was young.

In the wheelchair, getting ready to go home from the hospital, in spite of my son's clean bill of health, I felt the first pang of fear, a gnawing in the chest: how was I going to take care of this newborn, of this baby? The thought of placing the car seat appropriately in the car seemed overwhelming. I was extremely grateful that he latched easily on to my breast to feed amidst the horror stories of those mothers who had to hire breastfeeding specialists to help them at home. Yet the truth was I didn't even know how to bathe a newborn. I had no clue of how to space out his meals, his naps. Having had zero interest in babies and children prior to having him, I was not sure about when a newborn could safely be taken out of the house, or about teething or how to manage colic. I hadn't even known what to ask for at the baby shower and survived the ordeal thanks to the guidance and advice of dear friends.

Two weeks before the birth of the baby, a middle-aged woman, a humble, soft spoken Central American, started working at the house. Initially she was our housekeeper. Then, when the baby came, she moved in with us, and saved my life. Rosa, an undocumented immigrant from Guatemala, a woman who was abandoned by her husband who had promised her papers and a way to become legal, didn't say much at first. It wasn't long before she found her place at the house: a strong, reliable, all-seeing presence. Ever wise, ever appropriate, she knew exactly when to speak up and when to step back. A dutiful employee and a doting nanny, she was a watchful eye on "El Niño", as she affectionately referred to my son.

"Don't ever worry about him, Ana, I love him like my own." she told me one day, from the rocking chair in the baby's room, as El Niño lay in his cot, on his back, bedazzled by a sun, moon and stars baby mobile. In time, she would graciously open the door to her past, a starry night in the darkest, far away sky. With Rosa in the house, I was able to relax and take a deep breath for the first time in nine long months, which translated into newly found free time to meditate and ponder on things.

Rosa

How does one even begin to tell the story of one's personal savior? How does one tell the world about the person who has always been by one's side since meeting them, about the one who has been not only mother and grandmother but also companion and friend? One has to start at the very beginning, with all the anxiety, nervousness and fear that having a complete stranger move in with one to take care of one's child provokes. It was absolutely terrifying. In spite of having been brought with up with nannies and housekeepers, it was not the same. For instance, I didn't really know how to cook simple everyday things. Unlike my grandmother who had taught Tomasa, our cook, her recipes and sauces at the Big House, I was not in the position to teach Rosa how I wanted the food at home prepared and served for my husband and for myself, much less for a newborn. In addition, I had no idea how to properly clean a house since Rusty and I had relied on maids from cleaning companies that would come once a week to do laundry and keep the house clean and presentable. She was going to be the one teaching me! And teach me she did. Rosa, all four feet and eleven inches of her, we realized, turned out to be a formidable nanny/housekeeper.

She was born in Asuncion Mita, a small town in the western portion of Guatemala. She never knew why her parents separated when she was only two months old. She only knew that Rosario, her mother, had disappeared, unexpectedly, taking Rosa's twin brother with her. Rosario, Rosa was told, left in the middle of the night with the little boy swaddled in blankets, in secret, in silence. Unfortunately, the little boy did not make it. He died, of a fever, on the road. When Jose, Rosa's father, awoke the following morning, he found himself a single father and only care provider to a baby girl he did not want. As is the norm in Latin American cultures and societies, where women are expected to take care of the children, that same afternoon, Jose knocked on his sister's door, in the neighboring town of Jalapa.

"Rosa, Big Sister, look at what I brought for you, a baby girl! You can name her whatever you want if you take care of her!" Rosa's aunt took one look at the baby girl, who the father had carelessly placed inside a plastic basket. It was mid-October and the cold was already coming, and the tiny baby was shivering inside the basket, naked, except for a soiled diaper and a dirty cotton rag that Rosario had left behind and Jose had put in there with the baby. "Let me keep her. I love her already. I will name her after myself, Rosa," the sister said, forever freeing Jose from any future responsibilities, both emotional and financial.

When Rosa was seven years old, and all the way through high school, she frequently saw her father come into the small Bodega (shop) that belonged to her adoptive mother where she would help out at the check-out counter. He came in at the same time, three or four times a week, with several folded bills of cash which he handed over in exchange for food, toys and sweets for his other children by a new wife not unlike my own father's attention and care for his "new family" which I had been forced to witness at those millionaire weddings of long ago. He never gave Rosa anything. He never even looked at her in the eye. She knew he knew who she was. He knew she knew, too. And, as is the norm in Latin societies, those silent sightings would be Rosa's sole experience of fatherhood. In the motherhood department, she came out a winner. Her adoptive mother was wise beyond her years and her instruction level. In spite of never having learned how to read or write, she could read people better than anyone and had an extremely well-developed level of intuition and sixth sense. She was very, very kind and even more patient, which made for an excellent mother.

On Sunday mornings, at the local evangelical church where the family attended, she would impress pastors and congregations by effortlessly and comfortably, speaking in tongues. One late afternoon after the service, back at home, a Jehovah's witness, a preacher, who had been born in Judea, Israel, visited the house.

"Good afternoon ladies," the preacher said, admiring the stuffed pinatas that decorated the narrow living room. Making and selling Pinatas for children's birthday parties was the only other source of income that the family relied on. "I noticed the sign on your door. Do you know what it means?"

Rosa and her mother looked at each other.

"No, not really." Rosa said. "My mother made it during the service, this morning, and told me to put it up for everyone to see. No one knows what it means, not even her. But she wanted it on the door, so that's where I put it," she further explained.

"Young lady," the preacher said, "your mother has written the words 'Christ is the Alpha and the Omega' in perfect Hebrew."

Rosa stared at the man "Sir, my mother cannot read or write in Spanish, let alone in foreign languages."

What the preacher replied to Rosa, that afternoon so many years ago, would forever stay with her, and upon listening to the story, with myself, too. "God's ways are beyond human understanding."

Rosa was an excellent student, a dutiful little girl who never hurt a soul. She was never able to bring herself to wring the neck of the hens that the family bought alive at the market, like her mother and her sisters were accustomed to doing, in order to make "sancocho de gallina", a rich chicken and vegetable soup that the mother made and the family loved.

When she turned fifteen, her birth mother came looking for her, wanting her to spend a few nights over in the next town, at the small house she was renting. After several days of explaining and convincing and after the initial shock of finding out the truth, Rosa, reluctantly, agreed. Her mother put her up in the guest bedroom. The bedspread had beautiful embroidered accents depicting roses in red, pink and yellow. The sheets were pink as well as the towels, which had a deeper hue. A powdery, floral scent floated around in the small room. The whole scene delighted all of Rosa's senses. She was grateful to have come to meet and make peace with her past. As Rosa grew more comfortable, Mother and daughter sat together, chatting, enjoying the cake the mother baked for the occasion and washing it down with sweetened coconut milk. Not one word was ever mentioned with respect to why she had abandoned Rosa, much in the same way not one word was ever mentioned by my mother about taking all those pills to kill herself.

It became dark outside, everyone slowly retreating to their homes and houses; the only visible light out on the street coming from a few scattered lampposts and small lights by the front door of some of the houses, signaling that corn tamales and tacos were available for sale that night.

"Goodnight Mamita," Rosa told her mother as she climbed up the stairs to her pink room.

"Goodnight pretty one," Rosa heard her mother say. She fell asleep almost immediately, in the warmth and comfort of the magnificent sheets and bedcovers. Exactly at midnight, she opened her eyes. She sat up, perplexed by what she saw.

Her bed was completely surrounded by candles, which her mother had placed and lit while she slept, in the darkness. All the candles were black. Rosa trembled with fear. She took out the small bible she always kept under her pillow and hugged it. In tears, she started to pray. "Our Father, who art in Heaven, Jesus Christ protect me, Archangel Michael come to me...."

That night, the Celestial Hosts must have heard her pleas, as she finally fell asleep, exhausted, the small bible on her chest, close to her heart. The following morning, there was not a single trace of the candle lighting. She washed her face, got dressed, and went down for breakfast.

The house was quiet. She heard the voices of young boys playing outside on the street, pulling rudimentary carts that they had made themselves. The boys would visit garbage collecting sites, pick up whatever piece of trash that still looked "good" and pile them up in the carts: rest of dinners that had been thrown out, torn pieces of clothing, shoes that looked very old and empty bottles that could be resold. A dog barked in the distance. Her mother was nowhere to be found. She raced back upstairs to get her bag and her books. Quickly, she opened the door to the room where she had spent the night. Her mother was standing there, her back to the door, just standing there, in silence. Rosa screamed. Her mother started coming towards her. There was a blank expression on her face. Rosa flew down the stairs crying on top of her voice. She opened the front door and ran outside. She ran for a long time, without stopping, without looking back. At the next town, she called her adoptive mother from a payphone. Upon rescuing her, mercifully, her adoptive mother did not prompt her for information. She just hugged her for a long time.

For the several days that followed, Rosa kept to herself. One morning, after a delicious breakfast of fried eggs and black beans, Rosa told her adoptive mother the story of what had happened that night at her Mother's house. The ever wise, humble woman replied, "Rosita, there is evil and there is darkness in this world. There are those who choose to work with these dark forces and the entities that rule over them. Rosita, let this be a lesson for you to always be on guard and to never trust anyone until you know them, or at least know more about them." Wise words, indeed.

By then it was clear that all thirst for knowledge and information about her real parents had been quenched. Rosa embraced her adoptive mother as her one and only true mother and was able to concentrate on her studies at the small college where she would earn a teaching degree. She loved children, of all ages, and all children loved her. The morning of her graduation, two job offers were already lined up for her. The ability to truly connect not only with children but with teenagers was one of her God given gifts. Becoming a mother was her biggest dream. But life, as usual, had other plans. The eve of her nineteenth birthday, wondering why her boyfriend had not come to the house to blow the candles on the Dulce De Leche cake and to sing happy birthday with the family, walking the two and a half blocks that separated them, she ventured into his house. His mother tried to gently stop her and dissuade her from going upstairs, to the young man's room. Rosa was unpersuadable and relentless in her quest. Giggling and laughter came from inside the locked bedroom. Rosa knocked on the door, firmly. "Augusto, is that you in there? Is that you? Who is there with you?" The laughing came to a halt. "Augusto, answer me, please!" Rosa insisted. There was only deafening silence. Rosa hid her face in her hands and started to sob.

"Senorita, go home now; there is nothing else for you here," the boyfriend's mother said, matter-of-factly. Rosa knew it was the beginning of the end. The love letters and the visits abruptly stopped. If she saw him at the market or down the street, he made every effort to avoid her, looking away or unexpectedly turning around and walking the other way. There were no explanations. No apologies. And people would not leave it alone. The unwanted attention from everyone, the questions, the looks on the street, the conversations that fell silent whenever she entered a room...until the day when everything stopped. Surprisingly, she felt a wave of relief as her mother told her the news: Augusto was engaged to be married, presumably to the giggling girl in his bedroom. The door was inevitably closed and she felt she could move on. The gossiping and the whispering were forever silenced when Rosa announced her decision to leave Guatemala for the United States. Her mother never wanted her to leave but Rosa's mind was set.

Two weeks' worth of clothing were tightly rolled and packed in a small pink suitcase. A light brown crossbody bag contained her passport, an identity card from the school where she taught, a rosary, six hundred dollars in cash and a small card, a Holy Prayer card depicting "Our Lord of Esquipulas". The crossbody bag was taken over to the local church to be sprinkled with Holy Water and blessed by the priest. "Our Lord of Esquipulas" is a wooden statue of Jesus Christ on the cross that the passage of time has turned pitch black. Carved in 1594, it is venerated at the Basilica of Esquipulas, Guatemala, a popular pilgrimage site where it has survived many natural disasters over the centuries with little damage. Credited with the miraculous cure of the Archbishop of Guatemala from a serious ailment in the early eighteenth century, the "Black Christ" is considered to grant miracles and healings to those pilgrims who pray and ask for His help. And the "Black Christ" listened to her mother's prayers and kept Rosa safe, albeit for a short time.

It was a short three-hour flight from Guatemala City to Miami, Florida. One of her friends, another Guatemalan girl, also looking for a change of fortune, kept her company during the trip. They decided to stay together, as Julia, the friend, knew a friend of a cousin who had offered her a place to stay for a couple of nights, and also a job interview by another acquaintance who was looking to hire a nanny. They were promptly picked up at the airport by a man who outside of "Good afternoon" said nothing else during the ride to the friend's house.

They each carried their own bag inside as the silent driver drove off. A middle- aged woman welcomed them inside.

"You are to share this room and, my apologies, also this bed," the woman said.

Rosa and Julia were very hungry by now. "Could we have something to drink?" Rosa asked.

"There is water in the kitchen and please don't touch anything else there" the woman replied abruptly. The girls realized they were in for a rough ride.

"And by the way," the woman continued, "It will be $300 to spend the night here." Rosa and Julia looked at each other.

"When is the interview for the nanny job? When is that person coming?" they both asked. By now it was clear that the interview was the only chance for any of them to get out of that house.

"Mrs. Alvarez will be here at 10 in the morning tomorrow," the woman answered, walking away.

Needless to say, that night was one of the longest nights of their lives. Without having slept a wink, they both went downstairs at the break of dawn to wait for Mrs. Alvarez in the small living room. At 10 am sharp, a young woman, wearing a blue pant suit and carrying a beige Coach bag showed up. By now, Rosa and Julia were exhausted, starving and desperate to get out of the "guest house'. Julia, who suffered from severe anxiety, had the interview first. Afterwards, she went upstairs to the guest room to calm her nerves. Rosa, who had strategically placed the "Our Lord of Esquipulas" prayer card inside her bra, went last.

As soon as the interview was over, Mrs. Alvarez told Rosa she had the job. Rosa almost passed out from the excitement and the hunger. Mrs. Alvarez bid a quick goodbye and signaled Rosa it was time to go. Rosa called out for Julia, in vain, to say goodbye. Her new boss pulled her by the hand as they walked out and away from the guest house without ever looking back. Rosa was to stay with Mrs. Alvarez and her two little girls for four years, until Mrs. Alvarez got a divorce and moved across the country to Seattle, Washington. The two girls were now eight and ten years old, respectively, and they both went on their knees to beg their mother to take Rosa with them to Seattle. It was not meant to be. Fearing for her undocumented immigrant status, Rosa preferred to stay put in Miami, where, at least, practically everyone spoke Spanish and she felt the "authorities" were more lenient towards people like herself.

Rosa found a job as a maid in a hotel on Miami Beach. Even though she missed interacting and taking care of children, she thought of herself as lucky because the pay was decent to good (she could afford to rent a room at a guest house nearby) and the job was easy. There were never any benefits as they paid her "under the table" because she had no legal status; but in spite of this, she got by. She eventually left that job because the other hotel maids, her coworkers, always stole the tips left by guests at checkout in the rooms Rosa had meticulously cleaned and taken care of. There was no way around this, Rosa discovered, as said coworkers, all Colombian, had formed a "sisterhood", a veritable Union of Workers which proved to be unbreakable. Rosa moved on to a different job altogether.

A friend had alerted her to a vacancy at a clothing factory. She was hired on the spot. This job was different to anything she had previously done in her life. For twelve consecutive hours, with a single thirty-minute break, Rosa sat in front of a sewing machine and pressed on the pedal. After a few hours, the noise was unbearable. It was also mentally dumbing. They tried her as an apprentice for thirty days, after which they decided to not pay her the owed wages, claiming that she had been "in training" and that she had used their sawing machines for free! At the end of her apprenticeship, she had sewn together over one hundred shirts and the same number of trousers, flawlessly. They still refused to pay her. She put in her resignation and left.

For the following seven years, Rosa survived cleaning houses and doing some gardening on the side. She married a fellow Guatemalan, an accountant back in their country who unfortunately was unable to validate his degree and practice in the United States. He earned a living working as a clerk at a hardware store. He proved to be a kind, thoughtful man who always remembered birthdays and anniversaries and frequently showed up with at least six oversized, gorgeous red roses for his wife. The flowers and the romantic attention more than made up for the lack of money. Rosa couldn't remember a time where she felt any more loved or fulfilled. They rented a room from a Nicaraguan couple in Sweetwater. Every day, Rosa rode two buses to get to Hialeah, where most of the families whose homes she cleaned, were concentrated. She walked from the bus stop to the houses, sometimes for forty minutes, each way.

It was at one of those Cuban households where she would come face to face with "Santeria," an Afro-Cuban religion where primitive, ancient spirits are worshipped. Brought over by the slaves, Santeria is not only a religion but a way of life. First of all, not everybody can be a Santero. It is something that is inherited from one's ancestors, and a gift that one must work hard at to fully develop. Those that are ignorant and incredulous insist that Santeria and its "trabajos" or "works," which are aimed at individuals, do not have an effect if the person whom the trabajo is aimed at doesn't believe in it. The truth is quite the opposite. The Santero priests are not only able to summon the ancient spirits of the different African deities, disguised as Catholic saints (commonly depicted on tall, colorful candles sold at latin bodegas all over the United States and at all the supermarkets in South Florida) but the spirits of the dead. These "Iniciados" or "Initiated" men and women, as they are commonly known, pay frequent visits to graveyards and cemeteries at night to excavate the grounds looking for the skeletons of the deceased. The

Santeros believe that once the bones are in their possession, the Spirits are at their service in exchange for rituals and offerings of all kinds. It is a binding situation for both parties until the Spirits are released and the skeletons are buried again in their proper resting space. Any kind of relationship between a Santero and a Major Deity is life-binding. If any of the Saints grants a Santero a favor, no matter how small, the Santero is indebted to the Saint/God for life.

Rosa had been working for a month and a half for a Cuban couple who owned a medium sized house and a pair of German Shepherd dogs. The dogs were very well trained and completely tame, and Rosa loved petting them. After their daily afternoon snacks (bacon flavored bits), Rosa would let them out onto the backyard where they ran around chasing each other's tails , wearing themselves out. The house had three bedrooms in total: a master bedroom; a medium sized room designated as an office and a small room in the corner. The small room, Rosa immediately noticed, had no windows. The first day on the job, she was given instructions by the owners to never, under any circumstance, open the door to the small room. "Am I not to clean in there, Madam?" she inquired. "No. Never. Some things are better left alone." Rosa nodded in agreement.

One afternoon in late July, at the peak of the hot, Florida summer, the dogs were running around the living room, seemingly begging to be let outside. Rosa refreshed their water dish and opened the sliding door. The dogs leaped outside, excitedly. She went back to the kitchen for a glass of water. The floors were immaculate and the laundry was completely done. She let out a sigh of relief, as the chores for the day were almost complete, and thought of making herself something to eat. A loud noise came from upstairs. It was a loud, hollow, single knock on what Rosa made out to be a wooden door. Her heart skipped a beat and she felt a little short of breath. "Stop. Calm down" she told herself, as she placed her right hand over her chest. A second knock interrupted her thoughts, this time louder and angrier. This time her heart went all out. She opened one of the kitchen drawers, picked up a sharp knife and ventured upstairs against all common sense. It was as if someone or something was calling her and she could not resist the urge to answer the call.

The house was quiet as she walked up the stairs, one foot after the other, holding the knife with both hands. As she reached the top of the stairs, she realized the knocking came from inside the small room, the forbidden room. Someone was knocking on the door from inside, wanting to be let out. Rosa opened the door. A life size statue of Saint Lazarus (an Afro-Catholic hybrid of a deity) dominated the room. Nine wooden trays, loaded with coconuts, different kinds of breads and tobacco, surrounded the statue. A single candle, in purple, and a glass of red wine stood directly at Saint Lazarus feet. Rosa stood by the entrance, frozen for what seemed like a very long time. Outside, the dogs started to bark, loudly and incessantly. Only then was she able to move. She threw herself down the stairs and opened the sliding door. The dogs kept barking and growling but refused to come inside. They were standing just outside the glass door, looking intently at something or someone next to Rosa that only they were able to sense. Rosa kept calling them to come in. "Bacon bits," she decided, "A handful of bacon bits will make them come in." She was standing by the kitchen counter, trying to take off the lid from the snack jar. It was as if it had been glued together.

At that moment, the dogs gave a loud howl. Rosa looked up as every door of every kitchen cabinet and every drawer started opening and closing by themselves, angrily. This went on for several minutes. Rosa sat on the kitchen floor, her eyes closed, shaking. She then knelt on the hard floor and started to pray: "In the name of Jesus Christ; in the name of the precious blood of Jesus Christ: Our father whom art in heaven, hallowed be thy name…" Suddenly, all activity ceased. Outside, the dogs went silent. She opened her eyes. Every single cupboard was closed. Every single drawer was in place. At that moment, the owner of the house walked in. In tears, Rosa tried to explain what she had seen. He stopped her, as if he already knew what she was going to say. "We told you some things were best left alone…don't say we didn't warn you. Its best that you leave now." Rosa picked up her bag and walked out, still in tears. The dogs were whimpering softly, in the backyard. A week later, she received her wages in the mail. Whenever she comes across a Saint Lazarus candle at the supermarket, she shivers, to this day.

After the supernatural incident, a series of unfortunate events followed. One could say everything went wrong, abruptly and unexpectedly. Was life trying to teach her some needed lesson? Was it a karmic consequence of letting her natural curiosity take over her better judgement that July afternoon in the small room? All she knew was that her husband started coming home later and later every day. Up until this point, he would only drink on weekends, in the late afternoon, always with one or two friends from work. Sometimes an acquaintance from the Salsa dance club where he took Rosa on Saturday nights would join them for their afternoon drink. Rosa began to smell alcohol on him every single night. To make matters worse, her period was late. She rejoiced at the possibility of being pregnant, despite some apprehension caused by her husband's behavior.

Two weeks went by and her period never came. A home pregnancy test gave the awaited confirmation. She had not said anything to her husband about his new drinking habits yet. She chose to approach the touchy subject in the frame of the hope and positivity she thought the pregnancy news would bring to the situation.

"Honey," she softly told him one morning after breakfast. "I am pregnant! You are going to be a father!" He almost choked on his café con leche.

After a coughing spell that seemed longer than needed to clear his throat, he finally said something. "Are you sure?"

Rosa did not even answer. She just looked away. It was clear he wasn't pleased with the news. Feeling there was nothing else to say at this point, she stepped outside. He left for the warehouse without even saying goodbye. By then, Rosa couldn't control her thoughts. Both her mind and heart were racing, and she was convinced she was going to die.

Then, she did two things: first, she called the people whose house she was supposed to clean that day and cancelled. Second, she ran to the local church and spent five hours kneeling, in prayer. She prayed for guidance, for a good outcome, for protection for herself and for the not-yet born baby. There was no one else she could talk to. All her family was in Guatemala. She was not even legal in the country. She particularly asked God to make her husband stop drinking. "Oh Lord, please, make him care about the baby" she prayed over and over. "Please, Lord, I don't want my baby to suffer," she repeated. She stopped praying only because her throat was so dry it hurt her to even talk. Worn out yet confident in her prayers being answered, she went home.

In truth, Rosa was not able to tell if the father-to-be felt any tinge of tenderness or paternal responsibility. In the ten weeks that followed, he rarely spoke about the baby and made no mention of arrangements for a house move they both knew was necessary given the expansion of the family. Ever fearful and distrustful, she narrowed down her group of friends to only one, Teresa, a sweet, quiet girl from Peru, also illegal in the country. It was Teresa who finally told her. Rosa's husband was having an affair with a very large woman from El Salvador who had three other children from another union. Teresa herself couldn't understand why a handsome, healthy, employed man could go for a woman like the Salvadoran.

Rosa left the "coffee window" where both women had gathered that afternoon and went straight to the hardware store. When she arrived, she almost fainted. The other employees at the store, aware of her delicate state, offered her a chair to sit on and some water with sugar. She couldn't believe her eyes. A morbidly obese, very short light-skinned woman was standing next to her husband. Rosa lost all sense of decorum. "If you don't leave this whore right now and come home with me, you will never see me again or the baby."

The husband looked at her, calmly. "You listen to me. If you go home now and let me be, I will stay married to you until you get your green card. Just let me be, leave me in peace!"

All the other employees and the few customers at the hardware store were frozen, silent. A young woman started crying. Rosa didn't know how she did it, but she gathered the strength to walk away, this time for ever. That was the last time she would see her husband. There were no conversations a posteriori, no phone calls. No marital therapy. That same afternoon, Rosa picked up her things at the rented room, and left. One of the ladies she worked for allowed her to stay at her house for a couple of weeks until she was able to find another room to rent. The word on the street was the Salvadoran had hired a Santero priest to make Rosa's husband fall for her, in spite of her physical appearance and much to his own detriment. He was forced to work two jobs in order to feed the woman and her three children. By then, Rosa became an insomniac. The inability to sleep would stay with her until the very end. She would drink gallons of chamomile tea, only to fall asleep for forty-five minutes and wake up again, anxious, exhausted. With Teresa's help, she was able to find a room.

The morning of her move, she felt a warm, wetness between her legs...God was answering her prayers in the best possible way. She had fervently prayed for her baby to be spared from any suffering. That morning, on the twentieth week of her pregnancy, God, in His Mercy took the baby home. The days that followed were a blur in Rosa's head. She came home from the hospital where they cleaned out her uterus and stayed in bed all day, staring at the ceiling. She didn't eat anything for two days. Teresa came to see her often and lent her the money to pay for the room. She truly cared for her friend, and seeing her practically lifeless, in bed, made her fear for Rosa's life.

"Rosa," she tenderly told her, "The lady where you stayed after you left your husband is very fond of you and told me she has never had a better employee at her house. She wants you to be a live-in housekeeper for her. Rosa, I think its best if you take her up on the offer. I will coordinate everything."

Rosa, who had her eyes closed all the time, shut off from the world, opened them for the first time that day. "I will come with you. Let's go." Her hard work and diligence saved her that day. She was, indeed, the perfect employee, an asset to any household. Slowly, her long lost joy and laughter were once again present in her life. This bliss, unfortunately, would not last.

A phone call came in for Rosa, early, one morning. Her boss answered and she could barely understand the woman at the other end of the line as the connection was very poor. She quickly passed the receiver on to Rosa.

"Hello, who is this?" Rosa asked hurriedly. She heard sobbing on the other side.

"It's your mother, Rosa. She bled from her stomach last night and lost consciousness. We rushed her to the hospital but her blood count was so low she suffered a major heart attack." The female voice continued, still sobbing. "They couldn't save her Rosa, they did everything possible...She's gone. I am so very sorry." Upon hearing the news, Rosa lost consciousness, falling on the floor.

She woke up on the living room sofa. Her boss was holding her hand. Both Rosa and her boss knew she couldn't go back to Guatemala for the funeral because she wouldn't be able to re-enter the country. It was a hard decision. Rosa loved her mother deeply. She also had nothing (no husband whatsoever to go back to) in Guatemala. Jobs were scarce. Everything considered, she was probably better off staying here and working. She would continue sending money and goods to her family in Guatemala. Once she made her decision, a lot of the anguish evaporated. She made up her mind to make a life here. She knew she was intelligent, well-mannered and pleasant, a very hard worker and excellent with children. Seeing all this, her boss gave her the opportunity of Rosa's life. One of her daughters, a lawyer, was pregnant and due to deliver within the next few weeks. Even though this young lawyer had hired a baby nurse to help take care of the baby, Rosa would act as an assistant to this nurse so she could get the necessary training in order to be able to take care of newborns.

This act of generosity on the family's behalf made a world of difference in Rosa's life. It certainly made her a thousand times more marketable in the nanny world, and it provided even more personal happiness and fulfillment. Once again, God was answering her prayers of long ago. The baby nurse was so impressed with Rosa's abilities and quick disposition that she wrote a letter of recommendation in spite of Rosa's lack of formal training. A few months later, Rosa took the letter out of her purse at her interview with us. Rusty and I read it with attention. She was hired on the spot.

Blessings may often come wrapped in sadness and our prayers may not be answered in the manner in which we think they will, but all dark moments pass and we should live in the faith that all will unfold as it should.

Going Dutch

I went back to work after the customary ninety-day maternity leave. Fortunately, I had been spared from postpartum depression, and having religiously exercised throughout my entire pregnancy, I had not gained any extra weight other than the prescribed nine kgs and fit back perfectly in all my pre-pregnancy clothes. I was lucky to have given birth to a healthy, gorgeous little boy who was well looked after while I was at work. My complete trust in Rosa's intelligence and goodwill allowed me the freedom to concentrate at work and do my job well. A few months later, my boss called me in his office. To say I was nervous was an understatement. I knew my entire face, particularly my cheeks had turned cherry red, along with the usual spot just below my neck, revealed by the wide v neck of the scrub shirt. I hated when my face turned red and I couldn't control it. Minutes went by and my anxiety level was so high I couldn't even catch my breath.

Ninety nine percent of our biggest, most disarming fears never come to pass. That morning, my boss, in his usual sharp yet suave manner, welcomed me into his office and presented me with a promotion! "Ana, you have been my vice chair in acting for as long as I remember. It is time that your effort and strong work get recognized. You never shied away from the hardest, most difficult cases and I look up to that. Congratulations! I already spoke with the main office and ordered new business cards for you. They should be ready next week. Thank you, Ana, for your work. You certainly deserve this!' I was drunk with happiness and pride and walked out of that office like a Hollywood celebrity with an Oscar figurine!

From a bird's eye view, at that moment, my life was perfect. A closer look at my relationship with my son's father revealed it wasn't so. The good news was that after so many years of not knowing, I was finally able to put a finger on the reason for my dissatisfaction. A dissatisfaction that bordered on mild depression and drained me of any energy and joy that my son's presence in my life and the recent promotion at work could bring me.

My alarm clock went off earlier than usual that morning and my eyelids were stuck together. I had to get going and I did not want to go. I daydreamed of using up my "twenty-four hour pass," a game that I had played with myself and with God since the horror of The Big House. In the game, God took a good look inside my heart, measured my level of discomfort and fear at that particular moment, and granted me a respite, an indulgence, for the twenty-four hours that followed. During this grace period, I imagined, God would graciously grant me the gift of unawareness. At the end of the merciful pause, I would feel as if time and whatever uncomfortable situation I had to face had passed silently, without leaving any painful residue or memory.

"Almighty Source, grant me this wish today." I prayed. I needed one of those daily passes badly. I needed to keep my eyes closed for twenty-four hours until it all went away. Then, I remembered I was on call that day, that I had to anesthetize a patient for open heart surgery and that said patient was probably already in the operating room holding area, demanding to know where the anesthesiologist was. I jumped out of bed and headed for the shower, admonishing myself for ever thinking that God would let me skip one day without the usual pain and discomfort of my everyday life.

In the end I came to the realization I had a void inside me that needed to be filled; an emptiness, a sadness surrounding my relationship. I had serious concerns about the viability of my marriage having spent the first ten years completely engaged in living the busyness of life, without investing the time or energy any long-term relationship requires to survive and thrive. There was only one thing we, as a couple, knew how to do right, and that was travel. We travelled well together. I was the intellectual author of the itineraries that piqued my curiosity and he took care of all the details and the technicalities. He was always ready to drive in any foreign country; I wasn't. We enjoyed staying at nice places, delighted in gourmet food and thoroughly enjoyed seeing the world. That was our only existing commonality.

Arriving home one day after an exhausting day at the hospital, "Where did Rusty go?" I asked Rosa, surprised upon seeing the empty chair in his office.

"He is off to the supermarket," she replied. "He wanted to surprise you with your favourite grilled fish, and look over here," she said while pointing at the kitchen counter, "he ordered cookies from the store that you so love, Cookies-by-Design!" My husband was not only a wonderful cook but a gifted baker with a sweet tooth. He made sure there was always a dessert in the house, bought or made. He loved making things from scratch. I once ruined an entire tray of bagels he left in the sink for the "dough to settle". He warned me repeatedly his bagels were "resting there." To this day, I still don't know why he put them there.

In spite of the warnings, I got up from the table to wash an empty glass in the sink and…absent mindedly completely forgot about "his babies," turned on the water and ruined his project. The art of communication was not our forte. It had never been. From the beginning of the marriage, I gauged an ocean of difference in how we each experienced emotion, and an abyss of separation between the things that stimulated us intellectually. My love for his parents may have been the only other commonality we shared.

Theirs was a true love story that endured over the years in spite of numerous moves to different countries across the world and the upbringing of three children. Rusty's mother, Pamela, was born in Chile, of Anglo Scottish ancestry but lived in Peru after the family relocated there at a very young age. She was a beautiful woman, of medium height, with crystalline deep blue eyes and porcelain skin. An expert in the kitchen, both in the sweet and savoury departments, she definitely passed her sweet tooth on to her children. While her English was impeccable, English being the language spoken at home, her Spanish had the melodious singing tones of the South American Spanish, which incorporated the Andean nuances, completely absent in the Spanish that I was familiar with: the one spoken in the Caribbean islands and the countries in the coastal portion of northern South America: Colombia, Venezuela and Panama. She met Rusty's father, Andre, in Lima, in the early sixties, when they were both in their twenties, after he was transferred from Aruba, where he had an administrative post at "Air Aruba", the national airline. It was love at first sight. He was tall, of a sturdy build and very handsome. He spoke four languages fluently and certainly commanded respect.

English, Spanish, Dutch and Papiamento (a dialect spoken in the Dutch Antilles, a mélange of English, Spanish, Dutch and Portuguese; spoken "on the streets", Dutch being the formal, accepted language at home and at school) were part of his repertoire. In addition, he had a very strong personality which complemented Pamela's easy going, relaxed, demeanor. She was the embodiment of kindness and graciousness; he, on the other hand, was a bit sterner and drier in his mannerism. Where he was a disciplinarian, she was a soft, forgiving hand. Not once during the time that I knew her did she lose her temper or her patience. There was an older daughter, Moira, a sweetheart, and a baby brother, Adrie, an adorable bandit. Rusty was the middle child. Even though Andre grew a bright red beard on occasion, Rusty was the only red-haired child in the family. I could only think of myself as extremely lucky for marrying into such a picture-perfect family and held secret hopes of having a red-haired child myself.

The first six years of Rusty's life were spent in Lima, Peru, attending English private schools with other well-to-do boys of English ancestry; many of which would reliably keep in touch with him over the years and spite of relocations. His father's next move took the family to Puerto Rico, where Rusty attended Catholic schools and did his First Communion and Confirmation. It was there that he developed a liking for Latin people in general, particularly for girls. The Latin, "more fun" ways were definitely an antidote for the rigidity and properness he continuously faced at home. He settled down well in the tropical weather and in the island's laid-back ways. Seven lazy, long years went by and his father was transferred again, this time to Curacao, Arubas's not-so-great sibling and neighbor. There was always conflict and bad blood between the two sister islands, Aruba being the most prosperous thanks in part, to the preference by the American tourists over Curacao. In spite of its uniquely arid climate and dessert like quality, the coastline was one beautiful big beach peppered by luxurious all-inclusive resorts, an effective bait for the average American tourist. Curacao, with its old, Dutch colonial style and its European flavor, was the preferred holiday destination for the Dutch tourist. Curacao has a historic flavor to it; it houses the oldest synagogue (sand floored to this day) in the western hemisphere, and a comprehensive, very well laid out museum about the world history of slavery.

The father announced it matter-of-factly over dinner one night, as the family enjoyed the first bite of "pastel de choclo" a typical peruvian dish that with its flavorful ground beef and golden sweet corn, was everybody's favorite; a comfort food that Pamela thought would surely sugar coat the bitter news. He also mentioned that all three children would be attending Dutch Schools and that he had already contacted special tutors to teach them Dutch, a Germanic, guttural language where the words seemed to get stuck in one's throat.

Rusty was already fourteen and not very interested in learning another foreign language. He failed the first year of high school in Curacao for the simple reason that, in spite of the intensive tutoring, he didn't understand what the teachers were saying. Once he mastered the language, he successfully placed in the HAVO (hoger algemeen voortgezet onderwijs) level, one of the two programs of selective secondary education in the Dutch schooling system that lead to a higher placement in college. There are five years in the HAVO level and its diploma is the minimum requirement for admission to the universities of applied science. The remaining top level program, VWO (voorbereidend wetenschappelijk onderwijs) takes six years to complete, its diploma granting access to research universities. Everybody in the family went through the ordeal of learning the harsh language, including Pamela, who in her free time from her job as a clerk at a department store in Willemstad, practiced phonation while listening to a language course on the record player.

I, also, learned it. Even though mostly everyone from the Netherland Antilles, (Aruba, Bonaire, Curacao, Sint Maarten, Saba and Sint Eustatius) is multilingual, whenever all the relatives got together, they automatically reverted to speaking Dutch. I did not like feeling left out and was always filled with curiosity about learning a language where the verb, the part of a sentence that gave meaning to it, went all the way in the end. No wonder official translators in the United Nations have to wait until the end of the phrase that is being said whenever someone speaks German or Dutch to begin translating into English!

Learning Dutch was not easy. Despite my fluency in French, English, and Spanish, the sentence structure in Dutch was completely different and the pronunciation, to put it simply, was very foreign. It was a true intellectual exercise. Having spent six months of arduous, concentrated studying on my own, I found an opportunity for a short, one week, immersion course in the beautiful, historical city of Den Haague, The Hague, seat of the Dutch government and home to the King and Queen, Willem-Alexander and Maxima, in addition to numerous civil servants and diplomats. A group of four adults in total spoke, breathed and dreamed in Dutch. No other language was allowed during the seven day stay at the language school. Anneke, our instructor, pleasant but militant in character, had the pleasure of coaching Queen Maxima, a native of Argentina, easing her passage into western European royalty. Liz, an English girl whose husband had been given a position in Rotterdam was the only other female pupil. Henri and James, the other two students, from Lyon and Edinburgh, respectively, enrolled in the course for professional reasons too. I was the only one who was learning the difficult language for sentimental reasons, one could say. Looking back, a red flag in the form of Rusty's lack of enthusiasm for the intellectual effort put forth by my love for his family was completely missed.

The mornings were dedicated to reviewing grammar, vocabulary and sentence structure. At mid-morning, the class took a short break for tea. Then we had our first conversation practice. Lunch was brief, followed by half an hour of free time, to perhaps go on a walk around the premises or review a lesson. The afternoon session consisted of listening to recordings with more conversation practice. At five o'clock we all had a headache and took another break for tea. Sometimes we took the old-fashioned bicycles that belong to the school on a ride around town, which I found particularly nerve racking, as one had to pedal backwards to access the brakes and I wasn't the most coordinated member of the group. At the end of the week, we had learned plenty.

I was fluent in basic Dutch and was very proud of my accomplishment. I looked forward to the family gatherings where I could put my new skill to use. Rusty's father, particularly, was fond of the idea of having a Venezuelan daughter-in-law who could speak to him in his mother tongue, and at last, I was able to make sense of a phrase in Dutch I had memorized earlier on without really having understood its meaning: "Al draagt de aap een gouden ring, zo is het toch een lelijk ding" which meant: "Even though the monkey wears a golden ring, it will always be an ugly thing."

A much-cherished connection was built a few years later, during one of our travels, on this occasion, a two week trip to Holland, with the goal of meeting all the family members who had emigrated to Holland from the Dutch Antilles and, unbeknownst to me at the time, also from Suriname, the smallest sovereign nation in South America. In preparation for the trip, I researched the origin of the family surname, Dennert. It all began in Stendal, in what used to be known as the Kingdom of Prussia, a conglomerate of territories originating in 1525, which comprised modern day Germany, Poland, Russia, Lithuania, Denmark, Belgium, Switzerland and the Czech Republic. It was there that Friedrich Wilhelm Dennert, Rusty's great-great grandfather was born.

A mercenary by trade, he was registered as one of the military personnel to the Dutch Colonies, and served in Suriname, where he eventually married and where his children were born. Suriname, a small country with one of the highest levels of population diversity in the world, this being a consequence of centuries of Dutch domination and long periods of migration, not only voluntary, but also forced, was one of the territories that the Dutch managed to keep in exchange for New Amsterdam, which under English mandate, would become the city of New York. Once slavery was abolished, laborers from Indonesia (Dutch East Indies) and India (through British collaboration) were recruited. In the early 20th century, workers from China and the middle east were also hired and brought over. Most Europeans left after the country attained independence in 1975. This diverse cultural heritage accounts for the multitude of religions, dialects, and even holidays still celebrated in modern Surinam, which are definitely unique: the Indian, Javanese and Chinese Arrival Days, when the arrival of the first ships is commemorated.

In 1916, three of Friedrich Wilhem Dennert's sons left Suriname for the promising riches of the new oil refineries in Curacao and Aruba. One of the brothers, Friedrich Samuel Dennert, Rusty's grandfather, went to Aruba to work for Royal Dutch Shell, a British-Dutch oil and gas company. It was in Aruba where he met his future wife, Antonia Catharina Marugg, born in Aruba of Swiss-German parents. She bore him four children, two boys, Hubert Richard and Andre Adriaan (Rusty's father); and two girls, Cleotilde (Tilly) and Glenda.

Even though I did not sleep a wink on the way there, once the plane landed in Schiphol, it felt as if I had had a good night's rest with all the excitement about meeting new relatives and being able to communicate in my newly acquired language. Nothing like a bit of stimulation in the form of new cultures and new sights to make the intellectually curious wide awake and ready to seize the day! Our first stop was at Om (uncle in dutch) Dirk and Tante (aunt in dutch) Tilly's, an elderly couple living in Wasenaar, a city located between Amsterdam and The Hague. In spite of their ailments and poor health (she had advanced Parkinson's disease and he suffered a severe, disabling case of rheumatoid arthritis) they managed to be perfect hosts that early afternoon in June.

The weather was still chilly which allowed them the freedom to dress elegantly in their own home. I marveled at the small size of their townhouse and the vertical, steep aspect of the architecture and design, as is the norm in Holland, where its inhabitants continually fight the sea for land, literally. Born in Haarlem, Om Dirk was not only a true intellectual but also a brilliant man. An engineer by trade, he was recruited by Royal Dutch Shell to direct their operations in the Antilles. The young man's move to Aruba was a turning point in his life. He would fall in love and end up marrying an Aruban girl, Tilly. Tante Tilly was a tall (five feet ten inches tall) and charming. She combined the ease of the island ways with the familiarity of the Dutch ways, a winning combination that certainly won over Om Dirk's heart. They got married, promptly, and had three children. The family moved around the world at the whim of the bosses at Shell, who would eventually transfer Dirk to the middle east. The Dutch consider that a life lived in hot climates and tropical weather makes for an inferior quality of life, and as compensation for the "trying" years spent in the "harshness" of the heat, Dirk got to retire very early in life, spending the last 35 years of his life in retirement, thank God and the Dutch government for proper pensions.

That afternoon at their house, Om Dirk took out his old-fashioned record player and played a record of poetry read in old, seventeenth century Dutch. I was mesmerized by the strong, masculine voice on the recording and surprised to discover it sounded a lot like modern day English!

"Yes it does sound like English," Om Dirk agreed. "You see Ana Maria, there is an unexpected, surprise like quality to life. Never forget this, Ana Maria, and learn to always be ready for the unexpected: learn to think outside the box."

Over tomato soup and gouda cheese sandwiches, we talked about the special exhibits at the Rijksmuseum, in Amsterdam, the largest collection of Dutch art and history from the Middle

Ages to the present day and my second favorite museum in the world, after Madame Tussaud's Wax Museum in Amsterdam, which I thought was way better than the original one in London. Afterwards, he took us upstairs to his "atelier," a small room dedicated to the hobbies he had adopted in retirement: building small, colorful, toy models, real working machines with the complexity of applied engineering, with light and sound; and his sketches and drawings, which usually graced the Christmas cards that he sent out to family and friends every year.

His beautiful handwriting and the blue ink from his fountain pen made me think of Delfts blauw (Delfts Blue in Dutch), the famous blue porcelain, that was inspired by Chinese porcelain brought over in the seventeenth century by the United East India Company, a private merchant enterprise that held a monopoly on all Dutch trade and shipping in Asia. The United East India Company changed many aspects of everyday life in Europe, introducing new products and ideas and making them widely available beyond the elite circles. It always amazed me how the Dutch, from such a small country could exert such big influence on the rest of Europe and the world, through colonies and massive import of exotic goods: spices from the Moluccas, cotton cloth from India, cinnamon from Ceylon, porcelain and tea from China and a fascination with Japanese Kimonos and Japanese Lacquered furniture. I had the pleasure of corresponding with Om Dirk a couple of times, and seeing his letters in the mail always put a smile on my face. Grateful to our gracious hosts, yet exhausted from jet lag, we bid our goodbyes that night, for the last time. I was never to see Om Dirk or Tante Tilde again. Looking back on that period of my life, I wish I had spent more time on the things that brought me pleasure and true joy, such as letter writing and exchanging ideas with likeminded people and keeping in touch.

Having also learnt about the life of Hubert Richard Dennert, Andre's only brother and Rusty's uncle inspired me to visit his grave. Dead at fifty-three from lung cancer, he was not only a physician, a prominent general practitioner in Aruba, but a man who later on served as an influential political leader and who was adored by people. His short life was marred by tragedy since the beginning. Unable to have children at first, his wife Dorotea underwent countless expensive infertility treatments. The home was finally blessed by sons and a daughter, after which Dorotea left him a widower. She died within months of a diagnosis of pancreatic cancer. Alone, with three young children to care for, he had a second marriage to a Dutch nurse living in Aruba that ended in divorce. This kind woman would later on take care of him during his protracted illness in Holland, spending the last days of his life by his side, tending to him medically and emotionally. It was a long, slow descent for him, drowned in scotch which only deepened his depression and despair, given the grim prognosis of his ailment that as a physician he very well understood. My father-in-law was deeply affected by the death of his brother and tears would come to his eyes at the mention of his brother's name. What better homage to Dr. Dennert, I thought, and to my father-in-law himself, than naming my firstborn, the first male grandchild, and first to carry the family name, in his honour?

The Netherland Antilles left their mark on everyone, for better or worse. Thirty years after Moira, the eldest child of the family had left Curacao for Holland, with her husband, Albert, a successful engineer, the legacy of so many unprotected beach days, spent in the blazing tropical heat of the Caribbean, with heavy coats of tanning oil and no real protection from the sun, became a devastating reality. After having a successful career in the hotel business in Europe in executive positions, Moira spent the last two years of her life receiving treatment for Malignant

Melanoma. The cancer, slow to advance but deadly, mercilessly robbed her of the beginning of the golden years. In the end there was nothing else to do but palliative care. She left two teenagers behind, a boy and a girl, and a heartbroken husband. The family gathered in Huizen, Holland for a funeral service that hundreds of people attended, to the surprise of her parents, who did not know the extent of the love and good will that Moira had spread during her life and was getting back right there and then.

I called Pamela the day after the funeral. It was one of the most difficult phone calls I made in my life. What do you say to a parent on the eve of her dead child's funeral? Tears come to my eyes as I remember her strength and composure, as she told me, many years ago, over the phone: "Anita, thank you so much for your phone call. I am happy to tell you that so many people, so many friends showed up for Moira; Andre and I had no idea she was cherished and loved by so many…it meant a lot to us."

As for the Rusty, the years spent in the Dutch Caribbean left him with an international flair and a deep love for boating and sailing. He was an expert sailor, able to faultlessly decipher the direction in which the wind blew and making all the necessary movements and adjustments of sails and masts to power up the boats in the sailing club. Fortunately, the terrible skin malady that took his sister's life spared him.

I played matchmaker for many years before finally realizing that Rusty and I were not a good match. Having spent no more than a few weeks together because of the restraints imposed by a long-distance relationship, we really didn't know each other well when we got married. It seems to me that we still don't. Lacking the basic foundation for a relationship, we were unable to grow as a couple. Our interests and goals were very different, and so were our communication styles. Speaking for myself, I didn't know what I wanted from a partner when I accepted the marriage proposal.

Sometimes life is cruel, but mercifully, there are always lessons that sooner or later we end up learning. Perhaps the biggest one is "Know yourself, know your partner" before taking big steps together. In the very end, Rusty gave me my son and for that reason, all the struggle and unhappiness will always be worth it.

***

In retrospect, love for travelling with one's spouse and fondness for one's parents-in-law is never enough to sustain a marriage and I found myself in a terrible predicament by year ten of our unconventional union. We never really knew each other after five years of a long-distance romance during which we barely saw each other. At the height of the loneliness and the sadness, and in spite of having had a son together, I finally spoke up. I told him I wanted us to separate.

"You are as unhappy as I am and you know it," I told him over a cup of tea.

He stared at the floor for a long time. The truth was that he was personally very unhappy. His office was an hour away from the house. Since he was employed by a Spanish company that sold agricultural and packaging machinery to the United States and his job required a lot of travelling, we thought working from the house and commuting perhaps only twice a week would make for a less trying situation. He did try working from the house, but at home he couldn't do what he did at the office. He was frustrated but felt he didn't have a choice because we had to live close enough to the hospital for me to be able to take call.

"I think we should separate." Finally, I said it. The pressure was automatically lifted from my chest and from my life.

"What about our son?" he uttered.

"Our son has two loving, engaged parents" I replied. "That's all he needs. Believe me, he won't know the difference. He will think that all the kids have two houses; mommy's and daddy's."

"And Lytton? Can I take Lytton?"

"Yes," I said, choking up. "You may take him." And we parted ways, in the shortest and friendliest of divorces. My mind went back to my own parents' dramatic and protracted battle of a divorce, realizing how much pain and damage could have been avoided had there been a measure of self-restraint on their behalf.

Every one of my friends was in shock. My brother and my uncle weren't. They knew me, and they knew my marriage was not working from the beginning. We finally told his parents. Andre was very upset. It turned out that Pamela, ever the wise, composed woman that she was, had an accurate, realistic view of our situation. "I am not surprised by the news. As a matter of fact, I always wondered how two people that had absolutely nothing in common could get married and stay together." She was very supportive of my decision. Mothers know best. Always. She has been a wonderful grandmother to my son.

I would eventually make peace with my failed marriage and the personal hardships brought on by the separation. I firmly believed that happy parents make for a happy child and we were not happy together. I thought my son had the best shot at life with emotionally stable and content parents. To this day, all this has held to be true.

An Only Child

"Your laughter is the most victorious sword,
Victor of the flowers, and the larks.
Rival to the sun, future of my bones,
And of my love"

– Miguel Hernandez

Not once did he cry at nighttime of hunger; not once did he cry because his nappies were wet. I would consistently wake up a minute or two before he did, mother and child in perfect synchrony. He was very thin and very long, with pink reddish skin and a perfectly round head. For the first three months of his life, while I was at home during maternity leave, he slept in our room, next to me, in his blue bassinet. In the mornings, I would pick him up and hug him and kiss his baby face and head a million times while I sang two little songs that I had composed for him; one had come to mind during one of his first baths; it was about how all his little body parts would become squeaky clean, like his squeaky yellow duck toy, once he came out of the tub. The other little song was a compilation of sweet, pet names that I had made up for him.

After his feeding I would lay him on his back, change his nappy and then massage his whole body with the best smelling baby lotion I was able to find. I would either continue singing for him or play classical music, the musical notes arranged by Mozart were believed to stimulate neuronal synapsis and growth. He would muster what seemed like a big smile as his big eyes tried to find mine. Sometimes I was so taken over by emotion and tenderness that I would stop singing for a moment to hold back happy tears and regain composure. He was my baby, my beloved son, my one and only true legacy, flesh of my flesh, blood of my blood. He was my inspiration and my reason for being, and I would do anything in this world to see him smile. How could any parent look at their child and not feel the same?

For the very first time, I was experiencing a new kind of love, a love that was so pure and absolute that it hurt inside: I was experiencing unconditional love. As I delighted in my son's smile, I thought of all the grown men, patients at the hospital, burdened with illness and disease, some from birth, others through poor choices and bad luck. I thought of these men who, once, many years ago, had been someone's "little boy," some young mother's joy and hope, every single one of them.

I thought of the fifty-two year old who I had anesthetized for a bladder procedure, who found himself in a nursing home at fifty after two major strokes. I thought of the seventy-five year old grandfather who had buried a son lost to pancreatic cancer, now in the hospital himself, for a tear in his aorta. Memories of a thirty-three year old alcoholic, former foster child in many homes and a bartender at some obscure waterhole in the city, his liver finally giving out, bleeding to death in the Intensive Care Unit at the hospital, came to mind. It was then that I broke down, no longer able to hold back the tears.

I cried for all those children in foster care, for the ones that were orphaned and never adopted; for the ones that experienced fear, loneliness and pain and cried alone because no one cared; for the ones that went hungry, the ones who endured mockery and bullying in school for their unwashed clothes and torn shoes, the ones nobody wanted, the ones who always played alone… "Why?" I asked myself. In time, the answer to my question would eventually be revealed.

In spite of countless hours spent getting to know Rosa, watching her taking care of the baby and listening to all her stories, it was not easy going back to work and leaving my son behind. After three months of intensive interaction with her, I was certain he was in excellent hands. Still, I longed to see him, hold him and kiss him all the time. I missed his little body and his toothless smiles. My only consolation was knowing that I was working to give him the best. Deep down, I also wanted him to be proud of his mother. Rosa was instrumental in my acquisition of mental fortitude when the time came to leave him. She would always remind me that a happy, fulfilled mother made for a happy child. "Ana, remember I'm not here on the weekend, rest up and get yourself ready for then."

The truth was that from the moment my son came home from the hospital, Rosa had fallen in love with him. That morning, when I walked in through the garage, holding him in my arms, fresh from the hospital, I saw her, standing by the entrance, holding a white box with a blue ribbon in her hands. She had a present for my son, even though she had not yet met him: a cute little outfit, a striped blue onesie, with matching little socks and a hat. She won my heart right there and then.

Against the advice of many, after Rosa had been living with us for only eight weeks, I hired an immigration lawyer and filed a motion to start the long, arduous process of making Rosa legal. Many criticized me, convinced that the moment Rosa would get a green card, she would walk out on me and the baby. I never doubted my decision to help her. Something inside me told me one of my life missions was to help Rosa, and by doing so, I was helping all of her family in Guatemala, as Rosa continuously sent money and much needed clothes, towels, sheets and toys to her relatives. Life in Guatemala is marked by poverty and lack of job opportunities. In addition, by making her a legal resident, I was contributing to her peace of mind and lastly, I would give her the gift of being able to see her family again, after twenty long years of self -imposed exile.

Fortunately, we did not have to wait long for our first appointment with the immigration lawyer. The three of us, the baby with us by necessity as we had no one to leave him with, sat anxiously in the waiting room. At this point, we didn't know if anything could even be done as Rosa had stayed in the country illegally for over twenty years. We breathed with relief when the lawyer told us that because Rosa had entered the country legally with a tourist visa, she stood a chance. The motion was started to claim her as a childcare provider. The lawyer informed us it would take seven years for Rosa to become a citizen.

"Seven years? Are you sure?" I asked angrily, in disbelief.

Rosa was the one who answered. "Calm down, Ana. These things take a long time...have patience; I haven't seen my family in twenty years. Seven years is nothing." I looked at her and at the lawyer, embarrassed at my impatience and my lack of humility. Evidently, life was presenting me, once again, with the lesson on Patience, which apparently, I had yet to pass.

In the end, it took nine years for Rosa to finally get her Green Card and another five for her American passport. My son was already in elementary school the day she received her Green Card and was able to go back to Guatemala for the first time after so many years. She came to my room, excitedly, one late afternoon and broke down crying. "Ana, my family and I have no way to repay you for everything you have done for me. I want you to know that I will be here for you and I will take care of your son, always, for as long as you need me. As for my family, if you want to take a trip to Jalapa, they will take care of you and treat you like royalty. Thank you, Ana."

We eventually made the trip to Guatemala with Rosa, several years later. We were treated like royalty, indeed. For one week, my son and I were the object of every single family member's attention. Not only were we driven around by a knowledgeable driver who shared with us bits of history and local custom; we

were given cell phones in case we got lost and we were presented with handmade multicolor tablecloths, placemats and hand
bags, which were not only beautiful but unique. The women
slaved in the kitchen cooking the most delicious foods and
desserts. They even had a belated birthday celebration for us!

Rusty proved to be a wonderful, hands-on father over the
years. He has provided amply for his son, financially and most
importantly, emotionally. Our son has partaken in many active,
nature-oriented trips with his father and his cousins on his
father's family side. They thoroughly enjoy road trips, scuba
diving, hiking and shooting together. Having had Rusty as the
father of my child has unquestionably proven to be the correct,
wise choice.

As time went by, I outgrew the constant self-doubt about my
mothering skills. I stopped second-guessing myself so much
when it came to decisions about my son after becoming aware
that if I paused for a few moments to calm and ground myself
before making decisions or reacting to situations, I usually made
the right choice, in responses and in actions. With me, my son
has traveled the world and has been exposed to different
cultures and ideas. With the advent of electronic communication, we are always in a long, protracted conversation, about life
situations, world events, human nature...and when we aren't
sharing our thoughts, we can be found playing with his beloved
dog, Misha, or playing board games, at which, to this day, he has
always beat me. He is growing up to be an engaging , self-
assured and highly emotionally intelligent young man.
Needless to say, I have never stopped praying: As a mother, I
pray for guidance, inspiration and discernment; I pray that my
son knows his mother and father love him unconditionally; and
most importantly, I pray that he always feels protected.

***

My boy stayed a single child. I wanted to make sure he would be the recipient of all my attention and my free time away from the hospital. I have never regretted this decision and I know that in my particular case, time will prove me right.

Quousque Tandem?
(How Long Still?)

In my second year as an anesthesiology resident, it was announced, at the senior class graduation, that I had been chosen as future chief resident, an honor rarely bestowed upon foreign medical graduates. The celebration was dying down, the voices and the noise softening, when the director of the residency program approached me. He pulled a folded piece of paper from his pocket, a letter, addressed to me. It was written by the wife of one of the patients I had cared for during my cardiac rotation.

It read:

"Dear Dr. Michelena, my husband and I wanted to thank you for the excellent care you provided him with surrounding his heart operation. Your touch was soft, your words were always kind. You did not miss one day of my husband's protracted hospital stay. You always came prepared, not only with the knowledge of my husband's daily condition, but also with the patience to convey all the information to us. When we first met you, you seemed minuscule, tiny, almost lost in your green scrubs, not looking one day older than a high school girl. By the following morning, you had become a giant, our protector: you had taken charge. I trusted you to take care of my husband's soul when his heart was artificially stopped during the surgery. I trusted you would shine your light, like a lighthouse, illuminating the darkness of his heart standstill (she was referring to the portion of the operation when the heart is artificially stopped and the patient is placed on cardiopulmonary bypass and kept alive by means of the heart-lung machine) I knew you would light up the way for him to return to us once the surgeon brought his heart back to life. You told us you were trained in a foreign system, in a foreign land. You never told us much about your upbringing or your family. Today, we wish to thank you for being more angel than human, for giving us your expertise, your kindness, your smile, and even though you never told us much about your parents, we rest assured that you must have had great parents, and we bless them for having had you. Sincerely, Mrs. A."

Silent tears of sadness came, tears of pride, too. Sadness for the parents that never were. My parents. Pride for the victor that I had become—had always been. Pride for every obstacle I had managed to overcome, defying all statistically logical endings to my story.

I was a fierce, courageous eagle, soaring on wings of discipline and self-sacrifice, of attention to detail and perseverance. I had taken every single misstep, every want and lack, every disappointment and disillusionment, and had used them like bricks to build the wall of resilience that surrounded me. The desire to do something useful and worthy with my life so that I could help others, along with the commitment I made very early on to be morally courageous, had sustained me. I had held myself to the highest standards, and I had never lost hope.

I felt keenly the debt I owed to so many who had helped me along the way, and I felt compelled to do right by them. But it had all come at a cost, a cost that was not for me to gauge at that particular moment, but which would come due with interest in the years down the line. The void, the hole in my core, impinged upon my happiness. In spite of my success, at that moment and for some time, joy eluded me.

***

I was already working as an attending anesthesiologist in the United States when my father, the Peter Pan of my life came, once again, to do some shopping for his family. As we drove around in the intimacy of my two-seater roadster, I found that at last, I had the will to confront him.

"Why did you abandon us?" I asked. "Why did you leave us in the hands of that crazy woman?" Only silence and the sound of the engine and the other cars on the road came in reply. I was not to be put off so easily this time. "Why did you abandon me?" I demanded, more steel in my voice. "Why did you leave me?"

This time, he answered. "I suffered a lot, too," he said. And that was it. That was all he would ever have to say. That he had suffered a lot too.

Like my mother, everything had always been about him. It still was and would always be. Even now, now that I was independent of him, a high-achieving adult and no potential burden upon him—still, he could say nothing that was not centered on himself. The excuses I had made up on his behalf—"Maybe he didn't receive love from his parents," or, "Surely he did his best"—fell away like desiccated leaves. No excuses could be made, either for my father or my mother, that could withstand the long and painful experience now that it was viewed in the clear, raw light of my adulthood.

***

Five years after my mother left Venezuela for the last time, in the apartment from which so many disturbing calls had been made in the middle of the night, the dentist died alone. He was ninety years old. My mother never said goodbye to him, never explained where she was going, or why she was leaving him, and she never contacted him again.

Unable to bring herself to have children, my sister found her happiness in taking care of animals. She dedicated herself to her dogs. After her divorce, she remarried one more time, but, sadly, it did not work. Her kindness and compassion, both for animals and for people, remain unparalleled.

As for my brother, he found some peace and stability out in the Midwestern portion of the United States. A full-fledged Professor of Cardiology at a young age, he married his long time Venezuelan sweetheart and they had two beautiful, healthy children.

Over the years, my brother and my stepfather grew very close. He got along better with my brother than with his own son. My brother took him for his last stay in the hospital as my stepfather could no longer walk, the result of a severe case of spinal stenosis. He became incontinent and had difficulty with his defibrillator. His kidneys stopped working and he was severely anemic. My brother claimed his mind was affected, too. During a visit, my brother took him around the hospital, one last time, in the wheelchair. My stepfather cried. My brother cried too, hurriedly and quietly, behind the wheelchair.

My stepfather died alone. Although she knew his time was very near, my mother did not go to the hospital that particular day. He died only a few months after the passing of his brother, a professor of pediatrics at Georgetown University. His brother died of prostate cancer. The two had feuded bitterly while alive, but in death blood proved stronger than trifling conflicts. Apart from his poor health, the thing that probably made him suffer the most after finding out his first wife had left him for another woman, was the knowledge my mother had been unfaithful to him, by secretly marrying another man in another country while still married to him in the United States, a revelation that left the family reeling but somehow still unsurprising.

My mother was overwhelmed by his passing. She just stared ahead into emptiness. There were no wailing tears or drama. There were no crazy phone calls to friends and family. She quietly disappeared in her bedroom for a protracted length of time. I did not go to the wake or the funeral. My brother and my sister went. I was afraid of not being able to display my love for her as would have been expected because even after I long searched my heart for some compassion and care in view of her situation, I found none.

Fifteen years after I last saw my father, I took a road trip to the so-called spiritual city of Cassadaga, Florida. During the three-hour drive, I was thinking to myself how, growing up, I had been nobody's favorite. My father doted on my sister, in his own frugal way. My mother never hid her preference for my brother, of course. My grandmother had been a bittersweet presence in my life. That day I was searching for something, closure, perhaps, or maybe only a better understanding of why my parents had not loved me. Someone had given me the name of a medium, a woman who claimed she could channel the spirits of the dead.

She conducted the channeling sessions from her home. That afternoon, as I crossed the diminutive porch of her house, I shivered. In the small consultation room, we sat across from each other. Closing her eyes, she began. Immediately, she raised her hands to her forehead.

"There is an older woman here", she announced. "My head is killing me! Oh, it hurts so much!" She looked distressed. "This older lady is heavyset. She tells me she is related to you on your mother's side of the family. She must have died from a stroke or a blow to the head, my head is pounding now. Was there someone like this in your family?"

Right away I knew it was my grandmother.

"Was your grandmother alive when your son was born? She is showing me how she carries him in her arms.

"No" I answered, disappointed, thinking then the spirit in question was not my grandmother's. "She died many years before he was born."

"Wait, wait," the medium said. A big smile came on her face. "I see it now. Your grandmother wants you to know you were her favorite. She held your son in her arms before he was born. When he was a baby she would play with his feet in the crib and he saw her and giggled with her. She wants you to know that she has always looked out for him, that she has always protected him and that she will do so until the end."

I stood up and hugged the medium, crying tears of happiness and gratitude. Happiness because I had been someone's favorite, gratitude for the love, the love of parents for their children, of grandparents for their grandchildren...The love that never dies and that I was surely a part of, at last.

The Lessons

Life is a master teacher and will present the lessons until one has passed the test. Life always responds if one shows up to serve it and to give to it. Most of the sadness and the tragedies we see taking place around us are the result of our own free will, of our ill made decisions and the lack of discernment by ourselves and others. Life makes use of these trying situations to bring out the best in us, enabling us to grow as human and spiritual beings.

Overall, one thing is certain: we are never alone. Life presents us with many opportunities and throws lifesaving lines, all the time. Many times, the sources of love that life offers us are unconventional, unexpected. They are hidden around the corner, waiting for us to discover them, at the right moment. It is important to always remember that ninety nine percent of our biggest, most disarming fears never come to pass.

The external mirrors the internal. Change must first happen in the internal realm of the mind, before it is reflected in our external reality, which constitutes faith: the act of believing without seeing. Anything and everything is possible. Things can change at the blink of an eye, as nothing is ever written on stone. God's ways are beyond our human understanding, but prayer makes a difference and may lessen or soften our accrued Karma.

Life urges us to master the lessons, to be of service. It wants us to be the gentle hand that comforts, the one that dries tears and offers hope where there is none to be had, the one that doesn't judge. It wants us to have more faith in others, to be courageous, to be less afraid. It asks us to lead with the heart, to be accountable yet forgiving; to always give others a second chance. In the end, life never ceases to support us. Nothing is ever the end of the world.

***

Sometimes at night, in my bed, before I go to sleep, my mind wanders back to when I was a little girl, afraid, in the white bedroom of my childhood, in the horror of the Big House; and one of the nannies would sit on my bed and stay with me, holding my hand, until I fell asleep.

Sometimes I can almost hear Nivea's laughter, our housekeeper at my grandmother's apartment, during the trying years of medical school. Nivea, who always comforted me; who laughed with me and also cried with me, trying to convince me it was never the end of the world, when life became more bitter than sweet.

I think of Rosa, of the selfless love and stability she gave me and my son. And I am immensely grateful to have received so much from so many.

At night, sometimes, in prayer, I whisper some words to all those pillars of love and support in my life. I know they are listening, in spirit, wherever they are. I say to them: "Know that nothing was in vain, and that had it not been for the tenderness and the compassion you showed me, I wouldn't be where I am right now. Know that nothing would have happened without you and that your memory will forever live in my heart and in my son's heart. Thank you. I love you. I hope I have made you proud."

***

"But the effect of her being on those around her was incalculably diffusive: for the growing good of the world is partly dependent on unhistoric acts; and that things are not so ill with you and me as they might have been, is half owing to the number who lived faithfully a hidden life, and rest in unvisited tombs."

—George Eliot

THE END

Made in the USA
San Bernardino, CA
29 June 2020